GOD'S
Favorite
HOUSE

If You Build It, He Will Come

TOMMY TENNEY

Fresh Bread

An Imprint of

Destiny Image® Publishers, Inc.
P.O. Box 310
Shippensburg, PA 17257-0310

ISBN 0-7684-2043-1

Library of Congress Catalog Card Number: 99-76297

For Worldwide Distribution
Printed in the U.S.A.

First Printing: 1999   Second Printing: 2000

This book and all other Destiny Image, Revival Press, Mercy Place, Fresh Bread, and Treasure House books are available at Christian bookstores and distributors worldwide.

For a U.S. bookstore nearest you, call **1-800-722-6774**.
For more information on foreign distributors,
call **717-532-3040**.
Or reach us on the Internet: **http://www.reapernet.com**

Dedication

I lovingly dedicate this book to my late grandfather, Rev. E.W. Caughron. He went to be with the Lord while I was writing this book. Affectionately known as "Big Daddy," he was truly larger than life. Going back to West Monroe, Louisiana, will never be quite the same. Big Daddy left a "big" void. West Monroe is mostly memories now. Places outnumber people. He will be sorely missed.

Endorsements

Tommy Tenney has done it again! In the same thought-provoking style of *The God Chasers*, Tommy challenges all of us to restore a passion for the worship of God. *God's Favorite House* is destined to be on the short list of Christian classics in years ahead.

C. Peter Wagner
Chancellor, Wagner Leadership Institute
Colorado Springs, Colorado

Tommy Tenney has rendered the Body of Christ yet another thought-provoking and motivating work! Unequivocally, *God's Favorite House: If You Build It, He Will Come,* is one of the most excellent writings on worship. The truths shared are simple, but very profound and empowering. This book is a "must-read" for those yearning to be a sanctuary for the presence of God. It will stir your heart to true worship and incite a greater passion within to know the Father as never before!

Dr. Kingsley A. Fletcher
Senior Pastor, Life Community Church
Research Triangle Park, North Carolina

The God Chasers was a book born out of a heart for God—His glory, His throne, and His presence. In *God's Favorite House* Tommy Tenney has done it again. If, before, you had no appetite for spiritual Reality, no hunger for God, and no genuine longing for the presence of the Almighty—then once you've read this book, with a humble and open spirit, you will surely know true spiritual longing.

Rev. Colin Dye
Senior Minister, Kensington Temple/London City Church

This book provides a clear challenge to those of us who lead the church in worship. Once we have read this, we will no longer be satisfied with merely providing a "good time of worship" for the congregation.

Noel Richards
Worship Leader

Do a thing long enough, make it into a routine, second guess what's going to happen, and you'll soon get tired of it. Is that possible with worship? Yes, it is. We can all talk up the reasons why we should gather for worship in homes and church buildings, special events and mega events. But is this routine? Routinely boring? Even if it is not so for you, almost certainly it is if you are part of the young emerging generation or those who love Christ, but find church and its music difficult.

Tommy Tenney has done a masterly job in ensuring that worship is full of life, contentment, joy, and adoration. It is much needed and has arrived at the right time.

Gerald Coates
Speaker, Author, Broadcaster

An avid reader in love with the world of books since childhood, I eagerly devour dozens of books every year. Yet one unique volume always captures my heart and emerges as the most cherished. That book lives on my nightstand right beside my Bible, and I re-visit it frequently throughout the year, gleaning fresh insights, inspiration, and challenge with each reading.

The God Chasers was my #1 book for 1999. *God's Favorite House* will likely be my #1 choice for 2000.

Thank you, Tommy, for shattering my traditions, convicting my complacency, igniting my passions, and challenging my highest calling to worship. The Lord uses your anointed writings to woo me into deeper places of intimacy with the Father and to press me to higher summits on His mountain. I'm forever addicted to Shekinah glory.

> Judy A. Gossett
> Worshiper
> The River Ministry
> Vancouver, British Columbia

For those who hunger for the manifest presence of God, *God's Favorite House: If You Build It, He Will Come* reveals strategic keys to ushering in His presence and providing a place for His habitation. As a gatekeeper, Tenney props the door open, allowing us to glimpse the glory of God, and challenges us to experience this in our own lives and communities by completely and totally abandoning ourselves to worshiping God. I highly recommend that you delve into this treasure, allowing it to captivate you and compel you to a wholehearted pursuit of God.

> Pastor Dutch Sheets
> Colorado Springs, Colorado

Tommy's call and passion is to see the Body of Christ come together and to see the presence of God come in a greater measure than ever before. In his pursuit for God, Tommy has learned, and now imparts to the Church, how to be a house that God wants to abide in. The house that God comes to is the house that He is welcomed in.

> Rev. Bart Pierce
> Senior Pastor, Rock Church
> Baltimore, Maryland

There is an old adage that says, "It takes a heap of living to make a house a home." What is it that gives God an "at home" feeling? It is certainly not an elaborate structure, for Ezekiel records that the presence of God lifted—vacated the premises—of the ancient temple. This book points to the pathway of His presence. As His presence is entertained, God settles down and is always at home in the midst of worship.

In the Scripture, there was the tabernacle of Moses, the tabernacle of David, and the temple of Solomon. One piece of furniture present in all three was the ark of the covenant—where the mercy seat was, where His presence dwelt. Of the three, the tabernacle of David may have been God's favorite earthly house. It was because the curtains were up, the ark was visible, the glory was manifest, and the worshipers were there day and night.

God is so jealous for His presence and for true worship; the ark of the covenant is the only earthly tabernacle furniture that we find in Heaven, where we will worship Him eternally. What He seeks now is a house—an earthen vessel—wherein His presence can dwell, His glory can be manifest, and there is worship day and night. Tommy Tenney's book, *God's Favorite House*, is the work of a God-chasing architect. Take the plans and build a house for Him in your own life. Hand me another brick—and let's get started!

Just the observations of his father,
T.F. Tenney

I totally identify with Tommy Tenney's passionate pursuit of the sustained manifest presence of the Lord Jesus. His writings echo the deepest, desperate cries of my own heart.

As with Tommy's book *The God Chasers*, so with this book *God's Favorite House*. The more you read his message, the more you'll be encouraged that if God has created in you this degree of intensity for Himself alone—and for Him to show up among His people in as much of His blazing glory as we can handle—then He will ultimately fulfill you and not frustrate you.

One of the strongest messages of this book, from my perspective, is that you won't care how much you may have to revolutionize your priorities and agendas, lose friends, or "lose face" in order to more fully see God's face. And any book that motivates us to go in that direction is of immeasurable value.

Joy Dawson
International Bible Teacher and Author

Theologians help us to understand theories and doctrines about God; Tommy Tenney inspires us to passionately desire Him. My friend Tommy is a man lonely for God. Like the woman in Song of Songs who must arise and go about the streets and squares looking for her beloved, Tommy's heart is always searching for His Beloved. He not only shares his longing, he imparts it to us in this wonderful book.

Francis Frangipane

Tommy Tenney's book, *God's Favorite House*, is poignant and heartbreaking, for we have been breaking God's heart. As Tenney so eloquently points out (which at times took my breath away by his scriptural observances), God wants His children to love on Him and spend time with Him. And we do that *only* when we worship. As Tenney asks, who is Church for? He succinctly and with Scripture points out that Church is for *God*. This book has the potential to revolutionize Church as we know it. It is a must read not just for worship leaders but for all believers.

Mike Bickle
Author and Founder of Friends of the Bridegroom
Director of International House of Prayer
Grandview, Missouri

"Why" was his favorite word.
This adorable and extremely inquisitive little boy approached life with an irresistible wide-eyed wonder. He would sit at my mother's (Dottie Rambo) feet as she would tell the

stories of Holy Spirit's voice prompting her to write songs like, "He Looked Beyond My Faults and Saw My Needs" or any one of the hundreds she's penned. While other children would be playing games in nearby rooms, he was a "God chaser" in training.

I remember sitting in his parents' lovely dining room and his gracious mother gently scolding him, "Tommy, let the grown-ups get a word in, sweetie. Someone else may have questions." But truthfully no one else's questions seemed as honest and poignant as his. I marveled, "What a remarkable young man."

For many years our lives never crossed paths until a friend placed a book in my hands and said, "Read it now!" I saw the author's name and thought, *This can't be little Tommy*. I flipped it over and saw the picture and laughed out loud.

Same eyes.

Same hunger.

The God Chasers became the book I gave to everyone I could think of. I've not only read it several times, I've preached it without apology. My philosophy is, "If it ain't broke, don't fix it." When I was asked to read the manuscript of *God's Favorite House*, it was mailed to me on the road in the middle of a very intense time of touring and ministering. Although I was honored, I was concerned I wouldn't have time to read it.

The first night I took it into my husband, Donny, and my bedroom in the back of our tour bus and ripped open the envelope, the presence of the Lord suddenly filled the room. There was a distinct fragrance I have grown to love, and tears of joy fell down my face. I read a few lines through blurred vision, then slipped quietly into the tiny bathroom to keep from disturbing Donny.

There was no sleeping this night. I would read and worship, read and worship. At last someone had written what we had been experiencing and crying out for.

In November of 1993 Donny and I and our entire ministry team were doing "carpet time" in a church in Florida. The Spirit of the Lord asked us two questions.

"Can I interrupt your life?"

"Do you have time for revival?"

Without hesitation or even thinking of the consequences we responded, "Yes." By July of 1994 our schedule had been placed in a shredder and a three-day meeting in Riverside, California, turned into 77 services. Our lives were forever interrupted. The last extended meeting was over 20 weeks in Sierra Vista, Arizona, where seven churches joined together and still join in a weekly pursuit of God.

Yet something in us is not satisfied. If you're hungry to be more hungry; if you're thirsty to be more thirsty...if you're passionate to be more passionate for God...if you're wondering why others just don't get it...this is the book you've been looking for.

Find a quiet room, take a steaming pot of herbal tea or coffee, two boxes of Kleenex, and make sure there's a large clean piece of carpet nearby. Get ready to experience the Glory without veils—"God's favorite house."

Dr. Reba Rambo-McGuire
Singer, Revivalist

This book is a blessing of God to the Church of Christ. It will motivate you to make deep changes in the way you live and in your devotional life. The passion for the presence of God, the power of worship, the transforming encounter with the Glory are some of the themes that pastor Tommy Tenney develops in a clear and inspiring manner. Tommy Tenney is a precious man of God and a prophet for this hour. His ministry is a blessing and his message is like a refreshing breeze for the spirit. Allow me to recommend to you this new book from among his other, rich writings.

Rev. Claudio J. Freidzon, Pastor
King of Kings Church, Buenos Aires, Argentina

This book gives insight into worship and how worship impacts all else about the Christian life that I never thought about before. It is likely to inspire and redirect the ministry of anyone who reads it.

Tony Campolo, Ph. D.
Professor of Sociology, Eastern College
St. Davids, Pennsylvania

I have had the privilege of knowing Tommy and often ministering alongside him during the last several years. I have often heard him say "I am not a prophet!" Tommy, however, *is* a prophetic spokesman to the body of Christ at this time. This *is* s season for the Body of Christ to rebuild the tabernacle of David. This *is* a season for us to overturn our own tables of programmed relationships with God and become a 'house of prayer' again.

More than the actual message Tommy preaches and writes, he is, in his love of God, a man for this hour of church history. God has many servants, but few friends. It's the friends rather than the servants the Master reveals His time and purposes to. Tommy is a genuine friend of God. And as such he is well suited to call the Church back to a vital passion to seek not merely the hand of God's blessing but His face of Glory. It is with genuine appreciate with which I highly endorse this book for the whole Body of Christ.

Marc A. Dupont
Mantle of Praise Ministries, Inc.

Contents

Introduction

Do you have fond memories of a house in which you grew up? What are those memories? Are they rooted in the literal building or are they connected to what happened in that house? I suspect that the only reason you remember a specific building with warmth is because of things that happened there: walking with your father, playing with your friends, being held by your mother. Recalling the happenings of home rather than the physical structure of the house is what would that make you "homesick."

If God were to get "homesick" for any of the "houses" of worship on earth, I believe that it would be David's tabernacle. He has placed it on Heaven's historic registry to restore and preserve—*not because of the beauty of the structure but because of the passion of the worship.* The events and encounters God had there with passionate worshipers are what endear the place to Him.

Two of the pillars in Solomon's temple were made of brass, but the "pillars" of David's tabernacle were people! God is looking for new building material that will match the pattern of old. He wants to rebuild His favorite house. Are you available? He could use another "lively stone," a worshiper after the pattern and heart of David.

This book is not about restoring the physical structure or the mechanical operation of David's tabernacle. This book is about restoring the passion of worship—the heart of David. Structure will follow passion, just like marriage follows love and a household is produced.

About the Cover

The illustration on the cover of this book may not mean much to you; after all, the picture on the cover is just a house. But to me it will forever be a home. I may be the only one who knows that the cover design includes a photograph of the actual house I lived in at 114 Slack Street in West Monroe, Louisiana. The house belonged to my grandfather, "Big Daddy" E.W. Caughron, before my mom and dad bought it. My remembrances of this house actually go back to when it was still my grandfather's house. The man standing in front of the house is my dad, T.F. Tenney. Because of the memories, this house means very much to me. I am making new memories in my own house with my wife and children now, but my childhood memories will always make this little house in West Monroe my "favorite house."

Chapter 1

God's
Favorite House

I didn't realize that God had a favorite house until the summer I took my family on a "heritage tour" of my childhood home. We had to go to my hometown of West Monroe, Louisiana, to see my grandfather anyway. Since we were already in town, on one hot Louisiana afternoon I piled my family into our van for a tour of the neighborhood and the house where I grew up.

Some people would say that there isn't much to West Monroe, but it is special to me because it was home. We lived in a white clapboard house at 114 Slack Street. The huge magnolia tree at one end of the front yard is still there (they are the best climbing trees for little boys) but the pin oak tree at the other end is long gone (those are not so good for climbing). Every street corner seemed to hold another poignant memory that I just had to share with my fascinated family as we drove past. I pointed out the place where their daddy went to school and described everything that happened along our tour route (completely oblivious to the barely stifled yawns from my audience).

When we pulled up in front of the house, I pointed out the ditch where the neighborhood bully, Clint, and I got in a fight after he called my sister a bad name. At the time it seemed like a battle of biblical proportions, but the short version of it is that I punched Clint in the nose and he punched me in the stomach, and we both went home crying.

I loved the house where I lived and grew up, and I naturally assumed that my children would love it too. It was obvious to me that no one was home that afternoon, but in north Louisiana towns we share a close camaraderie and an unwritten code that makes room for "heritage tours." I don't know who owns the home now, but I didn't really think anybody would be upset if the Tenney crew toured their former estate.

I Had Powerful Memories From My Favorite House

The grand tour began in the front yard (with enough stories about the front yard to take up a good 30 minutes). I had many nostalgic memories about what happened at my favorite house at 114 Slack Street, and I wanted my children to have their own sense of heritage and historical connection to that house.

We slowly worked our way around the house while I pointed out the most important historical sites and reminisced about life in "paradise." As we passed through the gate by the back porch, I told my children about the time the dog bit the delivery man. I had never seen a delivery man dance so skillfully with packages in his arms. My dog wasn't really a big dog, but he supplied just enough inspiration to motivate that man to do an award-winning high-step all the way across that backyard. Personally, I thought it was hilarious, but the delivery man wasn't too happy about it.

My Family Had Abandoned Me

I described the playhouse in the backyard and my homemade tree swing upon which my sister managed to fulfill my mother's prophecy by breaking her arm. I was really beginning to feel good about the tour when, about three-quarters of the way around the house, I looked behind to find that nobody was there. I thought, *Well, they found something really interesting, and they're still awestruck by it.* I had just pointed out the grave site where my sister and I buried our pets, so I thought that maybe they were overcome with grief or perhaps entranced by the pansy bed where my mom taught me how to plant flowers.

When I retraced my steps, I realized that my family had abandoned me. I admit that it was the middle of a hot Louisiana day with 95 degrees outside and 100 percent humidity, but didn't they understand that that was a small price to pay to be in paradise? The truth is that they were convinced I was lost in "la-la land." They had returned to the van where they had the air conditioner running full tilt. Their faces registered a state of absolute boredom while they argued over what audiotape to listen to "while Dad does his little memory trip."

I was offended. No, I was more than offended. *I was angry.* "What is the matter with you guys?" I said. "I'm trying to show you all these things..."

"We're bored..." interrupted Andrea, my youngest daughter. "Dad, this house doesn't mean anything to us," chimed in Natasha, my middle daughter.

For a moment, I almost expected to see lightning strike our van. After all, you don't talk about sacred ground that way. It was almost sacrilegious! Then my irreverent oldest daughter said, "Dad, the only reason this house means anything to you is because of the memories you have. *We don't have any memories connected to that house.*"

Then it dawned on me that my daughter was right. My family isn't necessarily interested in the house at 114 Slack Street in the same way I am. I can tell them stories about life in that house, but those tales are more than stories to me. They are my life locked in the memories of *my favorite house.*

Why Does God Want to Rebuild *That* House?

A few days later I was looking at various verses in my Bible when my attention was drawn to this passage in Acts 15:

> *After this I will return and will rebuild the tabernacle of David, which has fallen down; I will rebuild its ruins, and I will set it up.*[1]

I thought to myself, *I wonder why God wants to rebuild that "house"?* Why wouldn't He want to rebuild Moses' tabernacle in all its originality? After all, that was the first heavenly dwelling place built by earthly hands. Even grander than that, why wouldn't God want to rebuild Solomon's temple in all its splendor? Why did God say He wanted to rebuild David's tabernacle?

In that moment, it was as if I heard the voice of the Lord whisper to me, "Because this is *My favorite house.*" *What a statement! Why did He say that?* I wondered. God seemed to answer from my experience, *"Because of the memories."* I believe that God has some treasured memories of events in that tabernacle that haven't happened anywhere else.

This book is not about a mechanical reproduction of David's tabernacle, but about a rebirth of the passion that caused it to be built in the first place. David's tabernacle was less structure and more "event." Church today is more structure and less event. That's the difference between a "house" and a "home." That is also what made 114 Slack Street so vivid to me and meaningless to my children.

If the passion of David's heart can be restored, then God Himself will assist in the rebuilding process of the tabernacle (dwelling place). *He said so!*

Of all the edifices, structures, tents, and temples that have been built and dedicated to God, why did He single out David's makeshift shelter on Mount Zion and say, *"This is the one I'm going to rebuild"*? The answer to this question threatens many of our most cherished ideas about what "church" is and isn't, and it has transformed my life and birthed the message contained in this book.

David's Makeshift Shelter
Barely Qualifies As a Tabernacle

As I mentioned earlier, it is curious that God didn't choose to rebuild Moses' wilderness tabernacle. *It is the original recipe.* Moses' tabernacle is the beginning; it is the tabernacle concept revealed in its most primitive or purest form. On the other hand, many of us would choose Solomon's temple in all its multibillion dollar splendor. Why didn't God say He would rebuild that royal dwelling place for Himself?

David's makeshift shelter barely qualifies as a tabernacle when it is compared to the tabernacle of Moses, and certainly when compared to Solomon's temple. It amounted to little more than a tarp stretched over some tent poles to shield the ark from the sun and the elements. Yet God said, "I am going to rebuild that one." Evidently, *what is impressive to God and what is impressive to men* are two different things.

When God said, "I will return and will rebuild the tabernacle of David, which has fallen down; I will rebuild its ruins, and I will set it up,"[2] He makes it clear that *He* didn't pull it down. *It fell down on its own.* That also indicates that David's tabernacle was propped up in some way by man. How do I know that? *Nothing that is held up or sustained by the eternal God can fall down* because He never gets weak or tired.

God seems to be saying, "I know that David's tabernacle was a tabernacle of man, and that man's hands grow weak and weary. So I am going to begin a process that strengthens mankind and leads them back to the same house that David had. That is My favorite house."

God Has Never Been Impressed By Buildings

For some reason the Christian world has forgotten that God has never been impressed by buildings. Pastors and members who meet in simple or makeshift structures constantly battle for earthly recognition as a legitimate church in town. Probably some of the multimillion dollar, splendorous church complexes in that same town *battle* for heavenly recognition as a legitimate church. Our attachment to steeples and stained glass *can* get in the way of real worship. If given a choice, God prefers passion over palace! If you recall, David wanted to construct a temple, but God told him He wasn't interested. If you look closely at the Bible passages describing the dedication of Solomon's huge temple, you will see God saying such things as,

> *But if you or your sons at all turn from following Me...then I will cut off Israel from the land which I have given them; and* **this house** *which I have consecrated for My name I* **will cast out of My sight.** *Israel will be a proverb and a byword among all peoples. And as for* **this house,** *which is exalted,* **everyone who passes by** [the ruins of] *it will be astonished and will hiss....*[3]

When Jesus' disciples remarked about the magnificent beauty of Herod's temple in Jerusalem, He prophesied, "These things which you see; the days will come in which not one stone shall be left upon another that shall not be thrown down."[4] Yet God never said such things about David's tabernacle. In fact, He says just the opposite. He seems to be not saying, "*thrown down,*" but rather, "Can I help you *prop up* your tent poles once again? Can I help restore what time has stolen and what the weakness of man has allowed to collapse? I want to preserve this house—the memories of 'man-encounters' here mean much to Me."

We want God encounters but God wants man encounters, because encounters with His children affect Him. He will "rip veils" and interrupt time to visit with His kids. When I put my schedule aside to "have tea" on the floor or in the playhouse with Andrea, it makes vivid memories for her; yet it also makes treasured memories for me!

David Was Interested in the Blue Flame

The most powerful component of David's tabernacle began long before the actual tent was constructed. It began in David's heart while he was still a shepherd boy learning how to worship and commune with God in the fields. It came to full bloom during his campaign to return the ark of the covenant to Jerusalem. His campaign is important to us because it is also a picture of our journey to return God's presence to the Church in our day. The following passage from my book, *The God Chasers*, describes David's motives as the ultimate God chaser of his day:

> "When David began to talk about bringing the ark of the covenant back to Jerusalem, he wasn't interested in the gold-covered box with the artifacts inside it. He was interested in the *blue flame* that hovered between the outstretched wings of the cherubim on top of the ark. That is what he wanted, because there was something about the flame that signified that God Himself was present. And wherever that glory or that manifested presence of God went, there was victory, power, and blessing. Intimacy will bring about 'blessing,' but the pursuit of 'blessing' won't always bring about intimacy."[5]

God Felt Strongly About David's Pursuit of His Presence

Somehow David captured something of the essence of God, something that no one else seemed to accomplish. I don't understand how this all works, but I do know that *David's passion for God's presence is crucial–I just hope it's contagious*. Ever since that steamy afternoon in West Monroe, Louisiana, I've heard the hint from Heaven: **"If you build it, *I* will come."**

Remember that David is the only man described in the Scriptures in this way: "I have found David the son of Jesse, *a man after Mine own heart*, which shall fulfil all My will."[6] I am convinced that there are two meanings to the phrase, "after Mine own heart." The standard interpretation is that David was a man who was "like" God's heart or "whose heart was like" God's heart.

I also believe that David was a man who was constantly "*after*" God's heart. *He was a God chaser, a pursuer of God's manifest presence.* His determination to bring the ark to Jerusalem is living proof of his passion for the Presence. This second interpretation is supported by David's unmatched descriptions of his intimate spiritual walk with God in the Psalms.

I won't go into all the details, but there are many similarities between the tabernacle of David, the temple Solomon built, and the tabernacle of Moses.[7] The tabernacle of Moses and Solomon's temple featured three distinct enclosed areas: the outer court, the Holy Place, and the Holy of Holies.

GOD DOESN'T JUST WANT VISITING HOURS WITH HIS CHILDREN. HE WANTS FULL CUSTODY.

A great veil (a heavy drapery in our modern colloquialism) was stretched across the tabernacle to separate the Holy Place from the Holy of Holies where the ark of the covenant rested.

The ark was a gold-covered wooden box originally built by Moses according to instructions he received from God. Its lid was fitted with solid gold figures of cherubim (two angelic figures) facing each other with outstretched wings. The space between them was called "the mercy seat," and this is where the blue flame of God's manifest presence hovered (also *shekinah* glory). The ark, the mercy seat, and the blue flame of God's presence were always hidden behind the thick fabric of the veil.

God never did like that veil. He had to have it, but He didn't like it. When Jesus died on the cross at Calvary, God was the one who ripped the veil from top to bottom in the temple of Herod in Jerusalem. He ripped it in such a way that it could never be rewoven again. *He hated that veil like a prisoner hates his cell door!* It represented the wall, the dividing line that separated Him from mankind. Until that day on Calvary, God had to hide behind the veil to preserve the life of the fallen humanity that came to worship Him in His holiness.

I Am Tired of Being Separated From My Kids

Perhaps the missing ingredient is the key of favor: *David's tabernacle was the only one of any of these structures that had no veil.* This key can begin to unravel one of the most important pieces of the wisdom of the ages: **God really doesn't want to be separated from us**. In fact, He will do everything possible to destroy things that separate and hide Him from us. He hates sin because it separates. God went so far as to rip the "veil" of His Son's flesh on Mount Calvary. At the same time, unseen hands ripped the veil on Mount Zion, as if to say, "I don't ever want this thing rewoven again! I am tired of being separated from My children." *God doesn't just want visiting hours with His children. He wants full custody!* He "has broken down the middle wall of separation."[8]

Now we are beginning to pick up some clues that tell us why God liked David's house better than any other built in His name. Moses followed God's directions and built a tent or tabernacle with suspended tent walls surrounded by a 15-foot-high linen wall on a wooden framework around its outside perimeter. In contrast, there was no veil and no walls of any kind around David's makeshift tabernacle. Nothing separated mankind from God's blue flame in David's house. In fact, *the only thing encircling God's presence in David's tabernacle were the worshipers* who ministered to Him 24 hours a day, 7 days a week, 365 days a year for an estimated 36 years!

During that time, if King David arose in the middle of the night with royal insomnia, he could hear the chanting, singing, and tingling of the cymbals coming from the tabernacle. He could look toward the hillside adjacent to his quarters and see the shadows of shuffling feet dancing around the ark, illuminated by flickering candlelight and lamps.

Perhaps it was a time like this when he penned:

Bless the Lord, all you servants of the Lord, who by night stand in the house of the Lord! Lift up your hands in the sanctuary, and bless the Lord.[9]

Day and night the worshipers stood, danced, and worshiped in the presence of God. *It is as if they were holding open the heavens with their upraised hands.* If David would look hard enough, if the angle was just right and if the worshipers would move just so, he could see the blue glow of the glory of God radiating between their outstretched arms and dancing feet.

In David's Tabernacle the Glory of God Was Seen By Everyone

David's tabernacle was unique. In every other place of worship where the ark of the covenant was housed, worshipers had to worship what was behind the veil without ever knowing or seeing exactly what was there. Only the high priest could venture behind that veil—and even then just once a year. But in David's tabernacle the glory of God was seen by everyone— whether they were worshipers, passersby, or heathens. *Unveiled worship created unhindered view!*

The miracle of "God's favorite house" can be traced to David's desire for God's presence. He said, "How can I get the ark of God to me?" He acted on that desire with all his being. His first attempt to bring the ark of the covenant to Jerusalem ended in disaster; it resulted in a complete overhaul of David's methods for "handling the holy." When David and his procession of Levites and worshipers finally reached Jerusalem after a grueling 15-mile journey by foot, David may have been dancing as much out of relief as he was out of joy: "We made it!"

Somewhere in the process of transporting that ark and honoring God, *David began to value the things that God values.* On the other hand, his wife *Michal valued dignity over Deity.* The curse of barrenness was placed on her, although the fact that she had no children could be attributed to the absence of intimacy with David.

Intimate encounters with God are sometimes embarrassing on the stage of man. The landscape of American Christianity is littered with barren churches who have turned their backs on the intimacy of worship. These are modern-day Michals who also have chosen to value dignity over intimacy with Deity.

Remember that David wasn't after the gold; he had plenty of gold. He wasn't after the box; he could have other boxes built. David wasn't interested in the artifacts in the box; they were nice mementos of God's appearance to others long before he was born, but they held no fascination for him. David was after that blue flame of God's glory. By his actions, David was saying, "I have to learn how to carry that blue flame."

We can build nicer buildings, raise up larger choirs, write better music, and preach greater sermons—we can do everything with more excellence than before. But if we are not carrying the "blue flame," then God isn't pleased. And He'll see to it that "flame-less" churches become as unimportant to men as they are to Him. No "flame" indicates no fire, which eventually results in barren buildings and hollow hearts. Somebody needs to say, "It's cold in here—that's why everybody's leaving. Let's turn up the heat of worship."

David Moved Beyond the Death-Dealing Separation of the Veil

Somehow David learned, in the process of handling the ark, something that helped him step beyond the limitations of the Aaronic priesthood and the priestly protocols of Moses. Somehow this shepherd-worshiper moved beyond the fearful, death-dealing separation of the veil into a new realm of intimacy with God. It changed his whole concept of worship.

When the exhausted Levites finally reached the temporary tent David had set up for the ark of the covenant on Mount Zion, David said, "You know, someday I hope to do something better, but right now this is how we're going to worship." The priests gladly lowered the ark from their weary shoulders and set it in place. But when some of the Levites began to walk off, David stopped them and said, "No, no, you're not leaving."

"But, David, we just walked miles with the ark on our shoulders. We've prepared and sacrificed thousands of animals to the Lord. Aren't we done yet? And besides, there's no veil or Holy of Holies!"

David told them, "No. I did not restore the Levitical office only to have the ark abandoned here like it was abandoned in Shiloh. Put your ephods back on. Get out your psalteries and your harps again. Some of you can go eat lunch, but the rest of you are staying right here."

"Well, who are we staying here for, King David? Do you want to listen to us play?"

"No, no. It is not for me—it is for God, an audience of One. He wants us to worship Him continually."

We Have Lost the Art of Entertaining the Presence of God

We want to attract God's attention, but once we get Him to visit, or once we sense His presence settle down among us, we say, "Hi, glad You came—gotta go," and go on our way. Too often we want just enough of God in our place of worship to give us a tingle or make a little chill run up our spines. We say, "Oh, He's here." The question is, "Will He stay?" It's not about us; it is about Him.

There has to be more to it than thrills and chills. David wasn't content to have a temporary visitation. He was after more, and that was why he told the Levitical worshipers, "You are not going anywhere. I want you and your group to take the first three hours. You guys take the next watch, and you take the third."

I long for the day when God's people will provide "24/7" worship to God, worshiping and honoring Him 24 hours a day, 7 days a week. With very few exceptions, church sanctuaries are the most unused rooms in America and around the world. While steady streams of people flock to 24-hour convenience stores to stock up on passing earthly needs, our churches can barely operate two hours per week because the demand for their "product" is so low. We must cultivate the lifestyle of "24/7" before launching organized structure lest it become like everything else we've done—*mechanical*!

This book is not written to advocate artificially propping open the church doors. It is a call to the passion of the heart of David, a worshiper. *His tabernacle became God's favorite house because of who worshiped there!* Just as 114 Slack Street became my favorite house, not because of the magnolia tree or the white paint and green living room carpet, but because of who lived there—Mom and Dad and the family.

God just wants to be with His kids. Stables will do—it worked in Bethlehem and at Azusa Street.[10] Anything to get close. If David looked at his humble tabernacle and said, "Someday I hope to do better," then God answered, "A tent will do, David. Just keep your heart hot!"

We have built beautiful sanctuaries with hardly anyone inside because, if there is no flame, there is nothing to see. There is no *shekinah* glory in our churches because we have lost our ability to *host the Holy Ghost*. Why did God say that He would build David's house again? I believe that it is because David's tabernacle had no veil or walls of separation. He longs for intimacy between Himself and His people; He wants to reveal His glory to the lost and dying world. He has to rebuild it because the weak hands of man tired of holding open the gates of Heaven with their worship and intercession.

Are we willing to rediscover what David learned, or are we already bored with God's "heritage tour"? Have we already slipped into the van and turned on the air conditioner while saying, "It doesn't mean anything to me because I don't have any memories attached to it"?

I wonder what it meant to God to be able to sit in David's rustic tabernacle in all His glory, to be seated right in the midst of His people without any veils or walls separating Him from His creation for the first time since the garden.

Turn your face toward Him now and ask Him what He really wants. The answer will change you forever.

Endnotes

1. Acts 15:16, referring to Amos 9:11-12 NKJV.

2. Acts 15:16 NKJV.

3. 1 Kings 9:6-8 NKJV.

4. Luke 21:6 NKJV.

5. Tommy Tenney, *The God Chasers* (Shippensburg, PA: Destiny Image Publishers, 1998), 38.

6. Acts 13:22b. This is supported by the original Greek text for this New Testament passage and by the Hebrew text for First Samuel 13:14, to which this quote refers.

7. Among the many excellent books on this subject, I recommend Kevin Conner's book, *The Tabernacle of David* (Portland, OR: BT Publishing, 1976).

8. Ephesians 2:14b NKJV.

9. Psalm 134:1-2 NKJV.

10. The Azusa Street revival in Los Angeles was started in a converted stable.

Chapter 2

False Finish Lines and Scented Doorknobs

Stopping Short and Missing Out

Some may call it blasphemy, but I must tell you that I have attended enough "good church services" to last me a lifetime. "Good" just isn't good enough anymore. I don't want to hear any more "good" singing and I don't even want to hear any more "good" preaching. In fact, I am bored with myself! Would you be interested in tasting something "good" when you know the "best" is waiting in the kitchen?

I know my comments sound extreme, but they are mild when placed in the context of what I really desire: I want God to show up in His *shekinah* or tangible glory. Compared to Him, everything and everyone else is reduced to a warm-up act filling time until the Real Thing enters the room. I am afraid that we have built a religion and a lifestyle around the appetizers while completely forgetting the main course!

We experience a taste or a fleeting hint of God's glory every time we find ourselves in places where what we call "revival" has broken out. Since this "glory" is a "spirit thing," it defies scientific definition or quantifiable verification. Instead there is a certain "feeling" or inner sense of God's approaching presence that warns us something very large and powerful is drawing near.

When this happens, we tend to handle the situation much of the time like inexperienced runners in a sprint race. We explode from the blocks in eager pursuit of God's presence and continue at a fast pace until we begin to feel the discomfort of an all-consuming hunt for the trophy of our heart's desire.

Some of us feel our strength failing and our senses becoming dull to things around us as we gasp for breath. With one last burst of desperate energy we stretch forward and lunge toward the line...only to stumble forward and fall several yards *short* of the finish line. By stopping too soon, by failing to press forward all the way through to the finish, *we are racing to false finish lines and fail to seize the prize.*

The Bible tells us that on a mountaintop in Israel, three disciples sleepily cracked open their eyes just enough to see Moses and Elijah standing with Jesus in a cloud of glory.[1] The disciples suddenly woke up and Peter interrupted the Son of God to suggest that everyone stop at the false finish line to build a monument to the event. Peter used the term *rabbi,* or teacher, when he spoke to Jesus, and he suggested building three separate structures as if he possibly felt that Moses and Elijah were equal to Jesus. Perhaps he had no idea that the best was yet to come.

Moses had waited more than ten lifetimes to see what was about to come to pass, and I doubt that he was interested in Peter's false finish line. He wanted nothing less than to see God's glory revealed. Then the Father interrupted Peter while he was still talking and corrected the disciple's earthbound perspective when He said, "This is My Son, whom I have chosen; listen to Him."[2] Then everything and every person faded from sight except the exalted Lord of all.

Too often we stop at false finish lines because our flesh gets excited. We want to interrupt God's revelation of Himself so we can build sand castles in honor of the first premonition of His appearing. We are so busy saying, "It is good we are here," that we don't hear God say, "I want to join you there too."

I Am Tired of Racing to False Finish Lines

It is no longer acceptable merely to have some good services, good music, and good preaching. We must meet God Himself. I am so weary of "almost" services that at times I tell people in our meetings, "If you came here for some good meetings, you've got the wrong model, the wrong preacher, the wrong place, and the wrong day. Come back another day. But if what you are after is God, then welcome to the brotherhood of the burning heart."

It was to the lukewarm church of Laodicea that Jesus said, "Behold, I stand at the door, and knock: if any man hear My voice, and open the door, I will come in to him...."[3] *The Holy Spirit is shopping for the place of the next outbreak.* He is standing at the front door of our churches looking for someone like David who has prepared a place for His weighty habitation—a place where worshipers are willing to prop open the door of Heaven with their upraised hands so His glory can come down and stay among them.

God is looking for a person, a church, and a city that will hear His gentle knock and open the door for Him. The Scriptures continually picture the Lord knocking on doors in both the Old and New Testaments. We see Him prophetically knocking on the door of His *own* house in the Song of Solomon, seeking the attention of His Beloved, the Church.[4]

Why would the door of His own house be locked? It is because He's given away the *key*. He told Peter the apostle, "I am giving you the key. Whatever you bind on earth is bound in heaven; whatever you loose on earth is loosed in heaven."[5] The Lord gave us the key to His own appearance when He *gave us the ability to open the windows of Heaven and close the gates of hell.* **The latch is on our side!** (But are the windows painted shut with man's traditions?) The Lover of our souls has persistently

Return to Passion Hunger for her 1st Love. open the door

knocked at the doors of His House, but we respond exactly like Solomon's bride:

> *I have taken off my robe–must I put it on again? I have washed my feet–must I soil them again?*[6]

God's betrothed Lover and Bride has become too comfortable. She refuses to open the door because it isn't convenient. The cost of intimacy seems too high. The discomfort of it all has bred an apathy that urges us to move too slowly and casually when our Beloved knocks at our heart's door. Ominously, the *knocking stops*—in alarm we finally rouse ourselves like Solomon's lazy bride. When we finally run to the door to unlock it, all that is left is the fleeting fragrance of where He used to be.

> *I opened for my lover, but my lover had left; He was gone. My heart sank at His departure. I looked for Him but did not find Him. I called Him but He did not answer.*[7]

This is the sad state of the overly contented Church today. We may find ourselves barren as David's wife Michal was. As we suggested earlier, could it be that David was never again intimate with her? The disgust she had for him locked the door to intimacy, joy, and fruitfulness. **The Church's reluctance to pay the seemingly high cost of intimate worship is the root cause of our barrenness.**

The Bride of Christ has grown accustomed to living in the King's house *in His absence*. If she would return to the passion and hunger of her first love, she would never be so content unless the King Himself were present with her in the house. Instead, the modern-day Church seems to stir just enough at the Master's knock to moan, "No, not now. Don't You see that I'm too comfortable to get up right know? Can't it wait? I have a headache. After all, I have already taken my shoes off and propped up my feet. Do I have to open the door for You right *now*?"

When the Knocking Stops

The most alarming time is not when God comes to knock on your door. It is *when the knocking stops*. Reality returns with a shock the moment it dawns on us that our Beloved is no longer knocking. We instantly forget the importance of our comforts and lounging lifestyle when the divine knocking stops.

> *I rose up to open for my beloved, and my hands dripped with myrrh, and my fingers with liquid [sweet-scented] myrrh, [**which he had left**] upon the handles of the bolt. I opened for my beloved, but my beloved had turned away and withdrawn himself, and was gone!*[8]

The Amplified Bible tells us that when the king's betrothed bride put her fingers on the bolt of the door, they came away dripping with the liquid myrrh left behind by the king. All she had left was the fragrance of where he used to be....

I'm afraid that if we don't open the door when our Beloved knocks, when the Dove of the Holy Spirit settles; if we fail to open the windows of Heaven through our repentant worship; if we remain unwilling to create an opening for God's glory to enter our world, then at some point *all we will have left is the fragrance of where He used to be*. Some are happy with that—they are content just to smell the fragrance or feel the tingle of where He used to be—but I am no longer interested in past visitations. What about you? *Vicarious visitations through the pages of history cannot satisfy me any longer. **I'm weary of reading about revival—I must meet the "Reviver."***

That reminds me of a grieving husband or wife who hugs the pillow and smells the fragrance of a spouse who is gone. Even when someone loses a spouse in the natural, the grieving process should come to an end in due time. The Church has memorialized the visitations of the past as if her Spouse has passed away and all future meetings (except the meeting in the sky) are out of the question. I'm sorry, but I don't want to cuddle up to the hollow memory of what once was! I want Him! I long to see Jesus in all His power, vitality, beauty, and glory. **Show me Your face!**

Would God Really Stop Knocking?
(It Has Happened Before)

It is time for us to spring up from our ivory couches of complacency to answer the gentle knock at the door. You and I are hearing that knock right now, but what bothers me the most is the fear that, at any moment, the knocking may stop. Don't think that I am proposing some new doctrine or odd interpretation of Scripture here. This has happened before!

During the "triumphal entry" of Christ into Jerusalem, people threw their clothing and palm branches into the street to pave the way for Jesus as He rode an untamed colt. The disciples shouted praises to God with new levels of passion and excitement, saying, "Blessed be the King that cometh in the name of the Lord: peace in heaven, and glory in the highest."[9] That really angered the religious Pharisees in the crowd because they rejected the idea that Jesus could be the Messiah.

When the Pharisees demanded that Jesus silence His disciples, He told them that even the rocks would cry out if He told His followers to be quiet.[10] His words as He looked out over Jerusalem describe what it is like *when He stops knocking*:

> *Now as He drew near, He saw the city and wept over it, saying, "If you had known, even you, especially in this your day, the things that make for your peace! But now they are hidden from your eyes. For days will come upon you when your enemies will build an embankment around you, surround you and close you in on every side, and level you, and your children within you, to the ground; and they will not leave in you one stone upon another,* **because you did not know the time of your visitation.** *"*[11]

> *I knocked and you didn't answer!*
> *I visited and you didn't receive Me.*

The Gospel of Luke says Jesus looked at Jerusalem and wept. I believe He wept with the intensity and grief of a spurned lover being rejected by his beloved. He said, "How often I wanted to gather your children together, as a hen gathers her brood under her wings, *but you were not willing!*"[12] I am not saying our salvation is in jeopardy; I am saying we could easily miss the moment of our visitation by the *shekinah* presence of God. We could miss the opportunity to give God that for which He longs the most—our intimate worship and communion.

Bartimaeus Couldn't See Jesus for Himself

Frankly, we all need to baptized with the spirit of Bartimaeus. This is the blind man who ignored the disapproval of the crowd to cry out to Jesus for mercy.[13] Bartimaeus couldn't see Jesus for himself. He was blind and had to believe in *blind* faith the testimony of someone else who told him, "Jesus is close." We must confess, "I'm blind and I can't really tell how close He is, but if somebody around me says He's near, then I refuse to let Him pass me by."

Remember this.

Sometimes the cares of the day and the weariness of life can temporarily blind us or so numb our senses that we can't perceive the nearness of God. That didn't stop Bartimaeus. Why should it stop us? When you can't see, feel, or sense the presence of God, that is the time to find someone you can trust who *can* sense His presence. When this witness tells you, "He's close, He's here," take them at their word. *Go for it!* Begin to lift your hands and cry out to Him by faith.

TEARS TURN ON THE FAUCET OF GOD'S COMPASSION.

Sometimes all you need to know is that He is near. Hungry cries from your heart will attract Him closer. After all, doesn't God's Word tell us, "The sacrifices of God are a broken spirit: a broken and a contrite heart, O God, Thou wilt not despise"[14]? God cannot turn away from brokenness. *Tears turn on the faucet of God's compassion.*

On the other hand, what happens when you know He is close and do nothing about it? Bartimaeus was just a blind beggar on the side of the road outside the city of Jericho, but he touched the heart of God with his hungry pleas while the people of Jericho evidently missed their visitation. You see, Jesus was *exiting* on the far side of the city when He encountered blind Bartimaeus. He had already passed through the entire city and nobody cried out for Him until He passed beyond the walls.

This begs the question, *"When He comes, will He stay?"* The people of Jericho missed their moment! Unlike the village in John chapter 4 where Jesus stayed several more days, Jericho's visitation was never turned into habitation. One blind man "saw" more than the entire city and delayed Deity long enough for a miracle!

Just Tell Me—Is That Him?

As Jesus passed through the gate, the blind beggar on the side of the road turned to someone standing nearby and asked a question:

"Is that Him? Just tell me, is that Him?"

"Yeah, yeah, Bartimaeus; that's Him."

"Then you better get out of my way because I'm about to lose my dignity."

Hear me, friend. *You can't preserve your dignity and seek His Deity. You can't save your face and seek His face.* At some point you are going to have to lose your spiritual manners. You will have to leave your Pentecostal, Baptist, or Presbyterian protocol behind you. You need to forget what you are supposed to do when, where, and how. You will have to reduce it down to the basics: "Is that Him? I think He's in the building! I think He's close." I don't know how you feel, but I refuse to let Him get that close to me and pass me by. "Jesus, Son of David, have mercy on me!"

Would Jesus pass us by? Absolutely. Jesus would have passed by the disciples when they were rowing a boat across the Sea of

Galilee in the darkness of the night, but *they cried out to Him.* He would have walked past the blind man, but Bartimaeus called out and kept calling out until Jesus turned aside to see him. Jesus would have walked past the woman with the incurable bleeding problem too, but she stretched out her hand and touched the hem of His garment by faith.[6] In the end, Jesus walked through Jerusalem countless times over the course of His brief life on earth, but the religious people of that ancient city missed the moment and the hour of their visitation.

One of the keys to turning visitation of the Spirit into habitation of the Spirit is recognizing Him. Has it been so long since you've "seen" Him? Would you recognize Him if He comes on a colt instead of a stallion? Would you embrace His visitation in humility as much as in power?

Would you believe me if I told you that Someone is knocking at the door of the Church right now? He is literally knocking at the door of His own house because He has given us the key. I don't want to see the Church miss her moment or hour of visitation. If somebody would ever open the door to Him, we won't be left to talk sadly about what He smelled like "the last time He knocked at our door." We will be walking with Him and fellowshiping with Him. Perhaps you sense something gripping your heart that makes you want to shout, "Lord, don't pass me by! Jesus, have mercy!"

"Father, I pray right now for a spirit of Bartimaeus to grip Your people. May we lay aside the garments of pride that identify us with the blind and lift our voices in worship, 'Jesus, Son of David!' We lift our voices in repentance, 'Have mercy on us.' We worship and repent and cry out, 'Don't pass us by!' "

YOU'VE NOT YET SEEN WHAT HAPPENS WHEN I VISIT A CITY. OPEN THE DOOR AND LET ME IN!

u forget about your manners right now? It is your religious protocols, the things that dictate 1 to happen and when. *God has always preferred over spiritual ritual.* Are you going to miss your 1 can feel Him edging closer and closer, then don't let Him get this close and pass you by, even while reading this book. Remember that *God is shopping for a place to break out.* He is knocking at the door. I can almost hear Him say to us, *"You know what happens when I visit a church. You've not yet seen what happens when I visit a city. Open the door and let Me in!"*

Put Your Hunger on Display

If there was a little baby in a church service who got hungry, do you think that baby would be impressed or bothered by the fact that Tommy Tenney is standing in the front of the room preaching? Do you believe that little baby would stop to think, "Uh oh, that is the pastor up there, I had better be quiet"? *If that baby gets hungry, things are going to get noisy.* Do you think that baby would worry about who is watching, who is listening, or what all the dressed-up adults are doing? No! *That baby is going to put its hunger on display* because all it knows is this: "If I don't get some nourishment or some help, I'm going to die." Do you think this is what happened in the Gospel of Matthew?

> *Then the blind and the lame came to Him in the temple, and He healed them. But when the chief priests and scribes saw the wonderful things that He did, and the children crying out in the temple and saying, "Hosanna to the Son of David!" they were indignant and said to Him, "Do You hear what these are saying?" And Jesus said to them, "Yes. Have you never read, 'Out of the mouth of babes and nursing infants You have perfected praise'?"*[17]

The Greek word translated as "crying" in this passage isn't referring to polite little cries of joy or soft sobbing. It literally means "to scream, to call aloud, to shriek, exclaim, intreat."[18] I think too many of us are just too concerned about the approval of men to pursue the presence of God. We need to become like starving little children crying for help.

*It's time for **you** to put your hunger on display.* Become like a little child and say, "I don't care who hears me. I don't care who sees me. *I've got to have You, Lord!* I'm so hungry." Display your hunger like Bartimaeus did on that miraculous day. Attract the attention of God and ignore the approval of man.

Even Little Babies Know When God Comes Close

Many times I will look across an audience when the presence of God seems to draw near and I'll see scores of small children weeping uncontrollably. I know I didn't say things to scare them, and nothing I said would appeal to their immature intellects. Yet even the babies in the auditorium know when *He* is approaching. They know when *He* comes close to the door, and so we see tears come trickling down their innocent faces. I usually take some time to reassure these little ones because I don't want them to be fearful. I just want them to understand that we're getting close to the gate. We are about to open the door for God to come in, and when you get close to that door you can almost feel the winds of Heaven whipping through your hair.

It's time to say, "I refuse to get this close and back off. *I'm not interested in false finish lines anymore.* I can't live another day with just the fading scent of God's 'yesterday presence.' I may not make it, but I'm going for it. I may not get His attention, but it won't be because I didn't try."

I really wish all of us would just forget our dignity and remember His Deity. Somebody needs to pray, "God, I'm going for it. I want an encounter with You *that I can't get over.*" If anybody ever does get Heaven's windows open, everybody will be blessed by the fragrance of His presence! If you feel you need to be in a church building and hear someone tell you the altar is open, then perhaps you are not desperate enough. Bartimaeus made his own altar from the dust of the road. Nobody told the woman with the issue of blood, "If you touch the hem of His garment...." No, she created a promise in her desperation and God honored it.

You can build your own altar from the hunger of your heart right now. I don't care whether you are sitting in the front pew of a church or the back booth of a bar or perhaps in your living room at home. It doesn't matter. It is time for everyone who is hungry to cry out to God,

"I'm not going to let You get this close and pass me by. I am desperate for You! Have mercy on me!"

Endnotes

1. Luke 9:28-32.
2. Luke 9:35b NIV.
3. Revelation 3:20.
4. See Song of Solomon 5:2.
5. Adapted from Matthew 16:19.
6. Song of Solomon 5:3 NIV.
7. Song of Solomon 5:6 NIV.
8. Song of Solomon 5:5-6a AMP.
9. Luke 19:38.
10. See Luke 19:39-40.
11. Luke 19:41-44 NKJV.
12. Luke 13:34b NKJV.
13. See Mark 10:46-52.
14. Psalm 51:17.
15. See John 6:16-21.
16. See Mark 5:25-34.
17. Matthew 21:14-16 NKJV.
18. James Strong, *Strong's Exhaustive Concordance of the Bible* (Peabody, MA: Hendrickson Publishers, n.d.), **crying** (#G2896).

Chapter 3

Opening Heaven
And Closing the Gates of Hell

The impression of the Lord came without warning while I was preaching a Saturday service at a church in Texas. In a moment of time, I just "knew" I was supposed to go to a certain city in another state Sunday night. The problem was that I was supposed to be preaching there in Texas that night also. I had never canceled a commitment like that, but I had to somehow accomplish what God wanted me to do.

When I told the host pastor of the church I was at that I wouldn't be able to stay for the Sunday evening service because something had come up, he was very gracious. At the end of the Sunday morning service, my hosts took me directly to the airport. (I felt such an urgency that I even skipped lunch.) The earliest flight was full but I bought a ticket anyway and waited as a standby passenger. I wasn't surprised when God intervened and I was given a seat on the plane.

When the plane landed, I rented a car at my own expense to drive to a church of about 3,000 where I had previously ministered. Along the way, God confirmed the decision by whispering, "You're on the right track."

I arrived in the church parking lot an hour before the Sunday evening service was scheduled to begin, hoping to meet with the pastor early so we could talk. I thought he might be able to help me understand why God told me to come at such a short notice and with no invitation.

As I locked the car and looked at the rows of parked cars, I noticed that a large number were already parked in the lot. *Well, maybe there is something going on,* I thought. This was confirmed when I walked into the building and noticed the ushers stationed at the sanctuary doors. They smiled when I approached them but they said, "We can't let you in."

Our Pastor Got Really Desperate for God

In my mind, it didn't matter how far I'd come or why because I believe in being under authority. So I said, "I understand that you can't let me in, but what is going on in there?" They replied, "Our pastor got up this morning and just got really desperate for God. He called a prayer meeting for four o'clock this afternoon and told us to close the doors after that time. It is supposed to go on until six o'clock, when the doors will open to the general public. It's only five o'clock now so we can't let you in."

"I understand," I said. "I'll just stay in the foyer." I found a seat near the door and began to pray with the people in the sanctuary from where I was seated. In a matter of minutes, the ushers looked over at me again and said, "We think you're a preacher." When I told them I was, they said, "Well, we discussed it. We think we're supposed to let you in there. We know the pastor said not to, but we really think we should."

All I said at that point was, "Probably so." When the ushers opened the door I walked in and saw about 400 people on their faces before God. I quietly joined them, and when the church service started sometime later, I sat in an inconspicuous place near the side of the room. When the pastor finally looked up, he spotted me and looked startled. Big tears were rolling down his face, and his tie was cocked sideways. (His attire and demeanor are usually immaculate.)

When the service started, the pastor and worship team seemed to be struggling because God's presence seemed to be so thick and heavy in the auditorium. A nationally known speaker had been invited to speak at the meeting, and when the pastor stood up to introduce the speaker, he said, "We have an honored guest here as our scheduled speaker, but I see my friend Tommy Tenney here." Then he said, "*I had a dream this week.* I dreamed that Tommy Tenney showed up here unannounced and uninvited. Now he's here. I don't know what God is up to, but I just want Tommy to come share something with us."

There Was a Good Chance God Would Upset the Agenda

I didn't know what God was up to either, but I knew there was a good chance He would upset the agenda for the meetings. As we passed each other on the steps of the platform, I stopped long enough to tell the pastor, "I don't know what's going to happen when I get up there." He looked at me with a deadly serious expression for a moment, without bothering to say, "Hi, how are you doing?" or "Good to see you." The spiritual climate was too serious for that. All he said to me on those steps was, "I don't care." I could tell he meant it because he was after God.

Ultimately, I would only speak to the congregation for about 10 minutes, but 15 seconds after I stepped up to the platform the windows of Heaven opened over that place. God's presence was incredibly strong, but it had nothing to do with me. It was as if God had asked for me to meet Him at this place and this time. And I was fortunate enough to show up for the appointment. In that moment, we were in "*the house that obedience built.*" The pastor had been obedient to cry out to God and call his congregation to prayer. The guest speaker was present and ready, and I had been obedient to come as well. God somehow lined us all up and moved us into the right place and position that night.

Within ten minutes people were literally running for the altars. (When God *really* shows up, I don't care what your title is or how long you've known Him, you suddenly become aware of the need to cover yourself in repentance. It is because of the weightiness of His approaching glory.) It was as if God just peeled back a place in the heavens and let a shaft of His glory hit that place.

As Duncan Campbell Said, "God Came Down"

The first person to reach the altar was the nationally known speaker, and the local pastor was right behind him. I watched people literally dive to the floor as they ran forward weeping and wailing before God. To borrow a phrase from Duncan Campbell's description of the great Hebrides revival, "*God came down.*" He just opened the windows of Heaven and showed up among us.

Every time this has happened in my experience and in Church history, "God came down" as a result of repentance and desperation in the atmosphere of worship. I can promise you that church programs will never accomplish this. *True revival comes when the Reviver comes to town!*

BROKENNESS ON EARTH CREATES OPENNESS IN HEAVEN!

True revival is more like a flood than a river. It is a supernatural explosion of God's presence in the earth over and above His continual omnipresence. Scripture says that "the earth shall be filled with the knowledge of the glory of the Lord, as the waters cover the sea"![1] How thoroughly does water cover the seabed? The "great flood" of Noah's day was a flood of judgment, but it may offer us clues about how the knowledge of God's glory will cover the earth. The Bible says that just before the great flood in the Book of Genesis, "...the same day were all the fountains of the great deep *broken up*, and *the windows of heaven were opened.*"[2] The New International Version says, "all the springs of the great deep burst forth, and the *floodgates of the heavens* were opened."

One way to release a flood on the earth is to release torrents from *two directions* at once—as in adding rain to an existing river. In the realm of prayer and revival, a way to open the windows of Heaven is to break vessels and release torrents of repentance and worship among the people of God on earth. There has to be a deep brokenness in us if we want to break through and see an open window in Heaven. *Brokenness on earth creates openness in Heaven!*

What Is an Open Heaven?

What do I mean when I talk about an "open Heaven"? An "open Heaven" is *a place of easy access to God.* We know from Paul's writings that there are at least three "heavens." He told the church at Corinth that he was once "caught up to the third heaven."[3] If there is a third heaven, of necessity there must be a second and a first heaven. The third heaven can only be the domain of God and His holy angels. It is the realm and "residence" of God. His rule from the third heaven affects the other heavens beneath it.

Since the Bible describes satan as "the prince of the power of the air," the second heaven is the dominion of the demonic.[4] The first heaven refers to the natural "sky" over our heads and the general dominion of man, or all that is within man's reach. Chapter 10 in the Book of Daniel provides a clear picture of all three heavens in dynamic conflict. When Daniel prayed to God from the first heaven, celestial conflict broke out in the second heaven between Michael the archangel and the fallen angelic ruler called the prince of Persia. God's answer to Daniel's prayer came through despite every effort in the dark realm to hinder or delay it. *Remember, delay is not denial.* Persistence plays a powerful role in opening Heaven.

What if Daniel had stopped praying after 18 days or 20 days? You must not let "brass heavens" deter you!

When we use the term "brass heavens," we are not saying that God cannot hear our prayers.[5] He heard Daniel's prayer and instantly dispatched an angel with His answer. The problem is that this angel passed through the second heaven where satan sent his own fallen angels to disrupt the communication. The adversary will try to stop your prayer from going up to God, and he will try to hinder the delivery of God's answer to you as well because the second heaven is his domain—*for now.*

Paul described satan as the "prince of the power of the air" in Ephesians 2:2. The adversary doesn't have complete dominion over the second heaven; he has limited dominion. He is only a created being and a fallen angelic prince. He can't even be compared to the eternal God and risen King. *A prince only has the power delegated to him by the king.* Our God has all power; satan the fallen prince only has the authority released to him by the King. There will come a day when even that authority will be stripped from him. Jesus has already stripped satan of the keys to hell and death.[6] *Satan doesn't even have the keys to his own "house"!* But he still has the "house." On that great day, God is coming to go one step further by "repossessing the house."

Do you want to see the windows of Heaven open up? Besides the biblical characters and their experiences, heroic figures from Church history also have left clues about opening Heaven. John Bunyan is one of them. His classic allegory, *Pilgrim's Progress*, may be the best known Christian book ever written, yet Bunyan didn't consider it to be his best book. His choice was a short book entitled, *The Acceptable Sacrifice*, which he wrote late in his life.[7] It is a book about brokenness based on an anointed exegesis of Psalm 51. Bunyan died while it was being printed, but he said that the book was "the culmination of my life's work." It was in Psalm 51 that David declared, *"The sacrifices of God are a broken spirit: a broken and a contrite heart, O God, Thou wilt not despise."*[8] This is **the costly key that unlocks the** *riches of God's presence!* This is the fragrance God cannot ignore. He will respond. The brass heavens will be broken!

David's Long Sweaty Journey Versus No-Sweat Revival

Christians around the world are saying, "We want revival; we want a move of God." Unfortunately, we haven't learned from David's mistakes. Often we try to do the same thing he did the first time he attempted to bring God's presence to Jerusalem. We cram the holy things of God on a new cart of man's making, thinking God will be pleased. Then we are shocked when we discover His disdain! He won't let oxen pull on carts carrying His glory! We expect somebody or something else to "sweat" out the hard part of revival. All we want to do is sing and dance in the procession. These half-baked, man-centered revival celebrations go as smoothly as David's first "ark party"—until we hit a God-bump at Nachon's threshing floor.[9]

These "speed" bumps on the road to revival may well be the hand of God saying,

> "No more of that! I will let you handle Me casually and cavalierly only so long. I will only let you handle Me with no sweat up to a certain point. However, if you really want to move Me from 'Heaven to earth,' you are going to 'sweat' it out. Don't try to transport My glory on your rickety man-made programs, methods, and agendas. You can have your cart or My ark—but not both!"

David retreated and did some research after Uzzah was struck dead at Nachon's threshing floor. *Uzzah died after he tried to stabilize what God had shaken.* We still insist on smoothing out the bumps and rounding off the edges of God's commandment. We are futilely trying to create an "Uzzah-friendly" environment when we prize man's comfort above God's comfort. I often put it this way: *"Seeker-friendly is fine, but Spirit-friendly is fire!"*

David discovered that God had told Moses that the ark should be transported only on the shoulders of sanctified Levites. God had had enough of man's ways, and He rocked the cart to let David's crew know about it. He didn't want anyone holding up what He was striking down.

Why would David put the ark on a cart in the first place? To the mind of man, it was logical to put a heavy box on a cart for such a long journey. Besides, that is how the Philistines did it. The ark of the covenant was a box constructed of gopher wood and overlaid with gold inside and out. It measured about four feet long, two-and-a-half feet wide, and two-and-a-half feet deep. The ark also had a gold top with two solid-gold cherubim mounted on it, and it was carried with gold-overlaid poles run through solid-gold rings attached to the side. Gold is one of the densest and heaviest materials on earth. Can you imagine how much the ark weighed? No wonder they attempted the journey on a cart! David learned the hard way that God doesn't think like men do. His ways—*and the road to a holy revival*—are higher and "sweatier."

Real Men Have to Sweat

When David made his second attempt to bring the ark to Jerusalem, he carefully followed God's instructions. God didn't want a cart of wood or an ox carrying His presence—He wanted real men. In fact, every six paces they would sacrifice an ox, as if to let both God and man know, "*No more oxen.*" The ox is a symbol of strength, power, and wealth. God will not be manipulated by our earthly wealth or physical strength. *The weakness of man is what will carry the ark of God's presence.* The Levites had to carry the heavy ark on their shoulders for a journey of an estimated ten miles. Those men must have sweated!

This process of bringing God's glory into Jerusalem is a symbolic picture of how we are to bring the manifested glory of God into the Church. (It is critical for us to remember the distinction between God's *shekinah* glory and His omnipresence, which is always in our midst.)

Obededom's house was somewhere between 7 and 14 miles away from Jerusalem, according to various theologians. By arbitrarily setting the distance at ten miles, we can form a picture of this process of sacrifice and travel to Jerusalem. The Levites would kill an ox and a fattened calf, move forward six paces, and go through the sacrificial process again.[10] Bible scholars are divided on this issue, but if David and his procession did stop every six paces to make sacrifices, then they put in some heavy labor on the road to revival.

Those Levites didn't put that heavy box on their shoulders and casually walk along for ten miles like they were taking a Sunday stroll in the park. They didn't walk through the gates of Jerusalem looking fresh and sharp in their "church" clothes shouting, "Hey, look at us. We're having revival!"

When You Seek God's Glory, Things Get Heavier, Not Easier

David and his procession of Levites, priests, and worshipers paid a dear price to usher God's presence into their city that day. It is no wonder that when that crew finally arrived at the gate of Jerusalem, *David turned into a dancing, spinning fool!* Why? They were thankful they survived the trip! I think everyone in the procession was shouting, "We made it!" Any way you look at it, this was a bloody, smoky process.

I believe it will be the same for us today. Hear me, friend: When you move from the level of anointing to calling for the glory of God to come, things don't get easier. *They get heavier.*

Most people go for the new cart method because it represents a low-cost, no-sweat method of worship. God warned Adam and Eve at the beginning of their life outside the gates of Paradise, "You are going to live by the sweat of your brow."[11]

"Sweat" has particular significance to God. It is the means by which value is transferred on earth. In modern terms, if you want to transfer money from the boss's account to your back pocket, you will have to sweat or labor in some way. In the same way, farmers have to sweat if they want to transfer value from the soil into their bank account to feed their families.

It could be that you "sweat" out a report in an air-conditioned office. Or you might drench yourself with literal sweat driving nails at a construction site. David understood this and refused to offer to God *things* that came to him at no cost![12] He would spend money he earned by sweating out the problems of the kingdom to purchase the ground and animals to sacrifice. He would also offer "sweaty" worship in the dance.

Sweat transfers value. It requires "sweat" to worship! Worship is actually "worth-ship," the transferring of value from us to God. That is why the giving of tithes and offerings are a part of worship. We transfer sweaty hours into dollars and then give sweaty money to God in an act of worship. This is just another way of transferring our "time" to Him. Whether you sweat figuratively or literally, you will sweat if you want to make a living. *And you will "sweat" if you really want to worship.*

When the flesh of our humanity gets lazy, we try to import or carry the things of God using no-sweat methods so we can walk along beside them and get all excited about "transporting the glory." The truth is that we don't want to sweat it out ourselves.

Are You Willing to Pay the Price for God's Presence?

Jesus Himself taught us to do exactly the opposite. He came to earth as a servant who made Himself of no reputation.[13] If you don't believe sweat has value, picture Jesus sweating it out in the garden of Gethsemane. Jesus moved His flesh into the ultimate position of sacrificial obedience to His Father's will when He "sweated it out" in prayer in the garden of Gethsemane. Things happen when you sweat out the flesh in your hunger for the Father. Eternal value is moved from here (your heart) to there (God's heart).

I'm concerned that most Christians aren't interested in paying any price for God's presence. We expect it to be brought to us on a silver platter. We are like spectators watching paid performers, or oxen, trying to drag God's presence into church. *It is time to abandon spectator-based services. Become a participator!*

Sometimes we do even worse. We play the role of Michal, Saul's daughter. We stare out of the windows of our religious palaces as royal spectators, making fun of those who get muddy, bloody, and sweaty in their sacrificial press for God's glory. Barrenness will always be the result of a lack of intimacy!

Am I talking about salvation by works? Absolutely not. *I am talking about the passionate pursuit of God*, the central theme that dominates the Bible narrative from Genesis to Revelation. I am talking about returning to our first love, *our first passion!* (Passion has become a dirty word in many of our intellect-centered churches.) Once we are saved and become His people by grace, we are to seek Him first, follow His commands, and live our lives for Him and not ourselves. This is where the sweat of obedient and repentant worship shows up.

The Robes of the Passionate Are Stained With the Marks of Bloody Sacrifice

The triumphant worshipers who entered the gates of Jerusalem carrying the ark of God's glory bore the marks of their struggle to acquire the blue fire of His presence. The ones who labor to restore God's presence and favor are easily distinguished from barren worshipers who stay in the comfort of the city waiting to see what will happen. The robes of the passionate are stained with the marks of bloody sacrifice. The mud and sweat on their priestly robes are visible reminders of their costly journey to bring God's presence from the threshing floor of preparation[14] into their city.

Does that mean that under the new covenant of Christ, we have to jump, hop, and skip to get literally sweaty so God's presence will enter our meetings? No, but we need to be willing to. God, who is Spirit, must be worshiped in spirit and in truth.[15] The self-sacrifice of Jesus Christ on the cross did away with the sacrifice of animals forever, but God never did away with the concept of *sacrifice* in worship.

As we noted earlier, David said that the sacrifices of God are "a broken and contrite heart." You make sacrifices to Him every time you sing hymns and put the virtue of your life into them. As I stated, another way you can "transfer sweat" into the Kingdom is through your giving. When you "sweat" or labor to earn money in the natural realm, you transfer part of yourself to God when you put that freewill offering into the Kingdom. You are transferring value.

Don't Offer to God a
"Sacrifice" That Cost You Nothing

Again, I believe that we need to learn what David discovered about the concept of value in sacrifice. Remember, he said, "...I will not sacrifice to the Lord my God burnt offerings *that cost me nothing.*"[16] He knew that the only way to restore God's presence and favor to his people was to sweat the thing out in sacrificial, repentant worship. *If the glory of God is going to come through the gates of the city, somebody has to carry it!*

Everyone who is pursuing revival today will tell you, "This revival stuff is hard work." Ask the ushers, prayer team members, and pastors who have to deal with a press of hungry humanity day after day and week after week in their overcrowded worship facilities. Or ask the intercessors who pray and pry at the cracks in the brass heaven. One man cannot carry the ark of God's glory all the way by himself in this generation. Others have to put their sanctified shoulders under the load on the journey to Jerusalem and say, "Here, let me help."

God Isn't Obligated to Feed Casual Nibblers

The way to open the heavens above you is for you to pursue a fresh revelation of where God is. We live with less than God's best most of the time because we tend to major on the truth of where God has been. This revelation must be pursued because God doesn't feed casual nibblers. He feeds the hungry. When He does reveal Himself to you or to me, that revelation will never take away from past truths; it will only add to them.[17]

Let me illustrate the difference between concentrating on past truths and seeking fresh revelation. If you were a skilled tiger hunter in India, you could tell me a great deal about your prey just by <u>examining its tracks</u>. You could probably tell me the tiger's size, sex, approximate age, and how long ago it made the tracks. In fact, you might even get very excited about those tracks because of the meaning they hold for you. *However, there is a vast difference between studying the tracks of a tiger and looking into the eyes of that tiger.*

Too much of the time, Christians become so enamored with the truths of where God has been that they fail to notice that He is visiting us right now. As I mentioned in *The God Chasers*, the Pharisees of Jesus' day were *inside* the temple praying that the Messiah would come, and they were totally oblivious to the fact that He was *outside* passing by them at His triumphant entry into Jerusalem! They missed their visitation because they were so locked into the prophetic "paw prints of the past" that they refused to recognize the moment of the Messiah in front of their eyes.

We all need to read and study God's Word daily, but we don't need to worship past revelation to the exclusion of all new revelation. Luther had a wonderful revelation of God's grace and he shared this "footprint of God" with the world. Once the truth of "salvation by faith" was laid down as a doctrine, men felt compelled to build a camp or shrine around that truth as if that was all there was and ever would be.

I believe that God is constantly giving us new revelations of His Person. This is partly because our unchanging God is continually moving and working among His ever-changing people. The ungodly part comes in when people begin to say, "Our paw print is the only track in the forest," or "Our revelation is the final revelation."

The Truths of God Should Lead You to the God of Truth

Always remember that *the truths of God are meant to lead us to the God of truth*, the Person of who He is. God wants you to follow these tracks of truth until you come to a revelation of who He is. **Thirty seconds of beholding the glory of Jesus through an** *opening in the heavenlies transformed a murderous Saul into the martyr named Paul. That's the power of an open Heaven!*

He began by following the Pharisaic tracks, but then he suddenly saw Him! Saul was faithfully following the old dusty footprints of the law that had turned to legalism. That empty legalism without revelation caused Saul to persecute the Christians who were following fresh new tracks of revelation. Saul thought he was doing what was right—until he saw the risen Christ for himself. Then he said, "I've had this all wrong."

I wonder how many more like Saul/Paul are out there just waiting on the Church to "open Heaven" so they too can have a life-changing encounter with the glory of God?

Honestly, if you ever have a real visitation of the manifest presence of God in your church, it will probably mess up your theology, destroy your structure, and change everything you've been doing! Why? Because for once you will experience His glory instead of simply studying where it has been. Frankly, this is my goal. I am in pursuit of the glory of God, and I want to open the windows of Heaven.

Making Smoke

Throughout the Bible, when the heavens opened and the glory of God appeared, a cloud was often involved. When God chooses to visit humanity, He brings His cloud for our protection. The cloud shields us from seeing too much lest we see His face and die.[18] We are close but covered. *When **you** choose to **visit God,** you have to make your own cloud.* Consider the Old Testament precedent in Leviticus 16 for any high priest who was chosen to come close to God's presence "behind the veil":

> *Then he shall take a censer full of burning coals of fire from the altar before the Lord, with his hands full of sweet incense beaten fine, and bring it inside the veil. And he shall put the incense on the fire before the Lord, **that the cloud of incense may cover the mercy seat** that is on the Testimony, **lest he die.**[19]*

A censer is a small container usually made of brass or gold that is often suspended on a chain. It is designed to make smoke when combustible incense is placed in the container along with a hot ember. *Prayer sprinkled on passion makes smoke.* Before the high priest would go behind the veil, he would put incense into the censer and thrust it through the veil with his hand. He had to make enough smoke to fill the Holy of Holies and hide the mercy seat before he dared to venture behind the veil. The smoke-filled atmosphere also forced him to perform his priestly duties by touch or by feel. He couldn't see anything! This was an Old Testament fulfillment of the truth expressed by the prophet Habakkuk and in three New Testament citations, "The just shall live by faith" (and not by sight).[20]

The Blood Gives *Access* to God; Repentant Worship *Attracts* God

The cloud of smoke was literally the priest's last layer of protection shielding his flesh from God's glory and certain death. It is the blood of Jesus Christ that gives us *access* to God's throne room today, but it is our sacrificial, repentant worship that *attracts* Him and allows Him to move *close* to us. In the same way, true worship makes enough smoke to allow Him to draw close to Him. Worship is the key component to the manifest presence of God coming down among us.

When you worship, you are "making smoke" as a sweet incense, a favorite fragrance, to attract His presence. If you make enough smoke, His mercy will cover you and God can come even nearer to you, and you can draw near to Him. The "worship cloud" releases His covering mercy so you can commune with Him in an intimacy and nearness that can't be created at any other time.

Mark the Memories That Stand Out About God

Think back through your life in Christ and mark the memories of God's touch that stand out. Can you recall what the preacher preached the time you had your closest encounter with God? Can you remember what the singers sang? Few of us can recall those details, but all of us can distinctly remember what God's presence felt like at that encounter.

It's like an encounter with electricity. If you have ever been shocked, you never forget what it felt like. *If He has even come close...you never forget!* I long for those times. I live for those moments.

The principle is simple: The more smoke you make, the closer you can get. Again, *the key is worship.* The value of worship is not measured in terms of volume and intensity. We know more about praise than we know about worship. Thanksgiving gets you in the gates, praise gets you in the courts, but worship takes you into His presence. We often get stalled in the courtyard and never make it to the throne room. Perhaps the low bow required when we enter the throne room and first see the King is a bit too humbling for us. Repentance has never been popular with the flesh.

The Word of God tells us that there are *five distinct and definite things that open the windows of Heaven.* This isn't a formula; it is a lifestyle of worship and dedication to God first in all things. All of the following are various elements of worship.

1. *Tithing* is an ancient key to the heavenlies that even predates the giving of the law to Abraham.[21] The principle of giving God the "firstfruits" of our income or increase is clearly described in the Book of Malachi:

   *"Bring all the tithes into the storehouse, that there may be food in My house, and try Me now in this," says the Lord of hosts, "If I will not **open for you the windows of heaven** and pour out for you such blessing that there will not be room enough to receive it."*[22]

2. *Persecution* also opens the heavens, as demonstrated in the Book of Acts when Stephen was martyred:

   *But he, being full of the Holy Spirit, gazed into heaven and saw the glory of God, and Jesus standing at the right hand of God, and said, "Look! **I see the heavens opened** and the Son of Man standing at the right hand of God!" Then they cried out with a loud voice...and they cast him out of the city and stoned him.*[23]

3. *Persistence* is an effective tool for "prying open" the gates of Heaven. Elijah prayed seven times and kept sending his servant back to search the skies until, on the seventh time, the servant saw a cloud the size of a man's hand rise from the sea. That tiny cloud from God grew into such a powerful storm that the skies were turned black with rain and wind.[24] Jesus told the disciples that the "door" would be opened to those who persistently ask, seek, and knock on God's door.[25]

4. *Unity* will open the windows of Heaven; it invites God's presence wherever two or three *agree* "concerning anything that they ask." Jesus literally said, "For where two or three are gathered together in My name, I am there in the midst of them."[26] The opposite side of this principle is illustrated in Peter's warning to husbands and wives to remain united so their "prayers may not be hindered."[27]

5. *Worship* is the fifth key to the third heaven. David the psalmist prophesied, "Lift up your *heads*, O ye *gates*; and be ye lift up, ye *everlasting doors*; and the King of glory shall come in."[28] Have you ever seen a "head" on a gate? It is obvious that David was referring to people as "gates" and "everlasting doors" through which the King of glory can come to the earth. This is a call to worship.

Like it or not, the only way we can begin to open the heavens over our churches and cities is to become giving, persistent, and unified worshipers who aren't afraid to sacrifice all for Christ.

Endnotes

1. Habakkuk 2:14.
2. Genesis 7:11b.
3. See 2 Corinthians 12:2-4.
4. See Ephesians 2:2.
5. See Deuteronomy 28:23.

6. See Revelation 1:18.

7. This book is very difficult to find, but copies are available from the GodChasers.network at P.O. Box 3355, Pineville, Louisiana 71361, and from our website, www.GodChasers.net.

8. Psalm 51:17.

9. The subject of the "bump" at Nachon's floor described in Second Samuel 6:3-10 is covered in much greater depth in Chapter 6 of *The God Chasers*, entitled "How to Handle the Holy."

10. See 2 Samuel 6:13.

11. See Genesis 3:19.

12. See 2 Samuel 24:24.

13. See Philippians 2:7.

14. I am making a reference to Nachon's threshing floor and the events that took place there (see 2 Sam. 6:6). The literal meaning of *Nachon* in the Hebrew is "prepared," according to James Strong, *Strong's Exhaustive Concordance of the Bible* (Peabody, MA: Hendrickson Publishers, n.d.), **prepared** (#H5225).

15. See John 4:24.

16. 2 Samuel 24:24 NIV.

17. Understand that I am in no way implying that we can "add to the Holy Scriptures." My point is that God wants to personally reveal Himself afresh to each individual, church, and generation. He never intended for you to go through life clinging to your grandfather's story of how God revealed Himself in his life 50 years ago. He wants to reveal Himself to you right now, and even more, He wants to "habitate" or relate to you continually day after day. He wants to make His Word come alive with meaning and fresh application to the situations unique to your life.

18. See Exodus 33:20.

19. Leviticus 16:12-13 NKJV.

20. See Habakkuk 2:4; Romans 1:17; Galatians 3:11; Hebrews 10:38.

21. See Genesis 14:18-20.

22. Malachi 3:10 NKJV.
23. Acts 7:55-58a NKJV.
24. See 1 Kings 18:42-45.
25. See Matthew 7:7-8.
26. Matthew 18:19-20 NKJV.
27. 1 Peter 3:7 NKJV.
28. Psalm 24:7.

Chapter 4

Building a Mercy Seat
Not a Judgment Seat

Some have been blessed with a visitation of God's presence and some have not, but all of us want more of Him. We welcome God's *visitation*, but our real desire is for *habitation*, where His presence lingers and lives with us every day. What can we do to make Him feel welcome all the time instead of just some of the time? We know that His will is for His permanent presence to bless our cities and nations, but how do we get Him to stay?

God spoke to me about this through a good friend of mine who has an apparent genetic disorder. This disorder causes him to be grotesquely obese. He can't be more than 5 feet 8 inches tall, but he seems to be literally as big around as he is tall. I've been told that when he was 12 years old he already weighed 300 pounds. He has struggled with weight all his life.

I remember times when we sat down together and he would start to weep, saying, "I know people laugh at me." This man has a strong anointing on his life, and he is one of the true apostles in the Body of Christ. God taught me something from an insight this man shared with me. I want to share it with you.

My friend is so heavy that it inhibits him socially. He told me, "I have very close friends who would love for me to come visit them. We regularly spend time together in restaurants, but I would love to just sit down in the intimacy of their homes and fellowship with them. Yet, I can't." He began to weep and big tears ran down his chubby cheeks. *The next thing my dear friend said would change my view of "church" forever.*

"Tommy, when I drop by their homes," he said, "I will stand at the foyer with my hat and coat on the whole time [it's usually cold in the northern region where my friend lives]. I never take them off until I scan the room. I've been there before." Then he looked at me again and said, "I've made my mind up. I've broken my last chair. *I refuse to sit in a seat that looks as if it won't bear my weight.* I won't be embarrassed anymore. I just won't visit if I have to do that. So I scan the room from the doorway."

"I hear my friends telling me in all earnestness and sincerity, 'Come in, sit with us, drink some coffee,'" he said. "The whole time I'm talking to them, I'm scanning their living room and kitchen to see if they have added any furniture this time that will hold my weight. I knew that there was nothing there during my previous visit."

Nothing in Your House Can Hold My Weight

With a sigh, my friend said, "Those visits often end in sadness because I have to make the excuse, 'Well, I need to go on, I can't stay.' The truth is that I'm only leaving because there is no furniture in their house that can hold me." He told me with tears in his eyes, "I usually get in my car and just weep. I go back again some time later in hopes that I will find something to sit on," he said. "*You would think people would look at me and know I can't just sit anywhere.*"

WE WELCOME GOD'S VISITATION, BUT OUR REAL DESIRE IS FOR HABITATION.

In the Old Testament, the Hebrew word translated as "glory" is *kabod*. It literally means weightiness or weighty splendor.[1] In a sense, God has the same problem as my friend. *I wonder how many times the "weighty glory" of God has visited us but not come in?* How often does He stand at the back door of our assemblies with His glory still hidden by His "hat and coat" while He scans the room?

We stop to count our spiritual goose bumps because we feel a cool breeze enter the room when the heavenly door opens. We tell one another, "Oh, God is here! He's visiting us again." Our singers rejoice and the band picks up the pace, but all too quickly it escapes us because we don't have what He is looking for. Most who have experienced visitations ask the question, "Why won't He stay? We begged Him to stay. Why can't we keep these moments?"

The answer is very simple: *We haven't built a mercy seat to hold the glory of God.* There is no place for Him to sit! What is comfortable to you and I is not comfortable to the *kabod*, the weightiness of God. We are happy to sit in our comfortable spiritual recliners all day, but the seat of God, the mercy seat, is a little different. It is the only seat on earth that can bear the weight of His glory and compel Him to come in and *stay*.

God is looking for a church that has learned how to build a mercy seat for His glory. When He finds a house that has paid the price to build Him a resting place, He will come and He will stay. That is when we will see a revival that is unlike any we have ever seen before. I am convinced that we don't even have a word for it. This kind of revival can only come when God comes in His weighty glory and takes His seat of honor in His house—to stay.

If You Build It, He Will...

When the Lord reminded me of my friend's story, my mind began to race. Another important piece of the puzzle had snapped into place. *We must learn how to build a mercy seat,* I thought to myself. Then I remembered the line from a motion picture I saw during a transoceanic flight that greatly affected me the first time I saw it. The motion picture was *The Field of Dreams*, and the line that came to mind in that instant was, "If you build it, *He* will come...," a lesson David learned.

The southern region of the United States is generally recognized for its "southern hospitality." Since I'm a southern boy, I thought I understood some of the basic principles of hospitality. I felt that way until God sent me, unasked, on a journey that led me to invest about 30 percent of my ministry among the Chinese that year. (I still minister quite often in mainland China and Taiwan.) He said, "I'm going to show you something about honor that most westerners do not know."

I learned that Oriental people have an ability to give honor that surpasses anything I have ever witnessed anywhere else. We practice hospitality in the West, but we are kind of casual about it: "Oh, hi. Come in. Sit down if you want to."

It is not that way with the Chinese. They are very careful to focus all their attention and energies on their guests. They put their guests' well-being first, and they work tirelessly to put their guests' comfort, peace, and happiness above their own. The way the Chinese carefully prepare in advance for their guests' arrival is an open statement declaring that those guests are highly valued and respected. They even carefully reserve the traditional seat of honor...the chair furthest from and facing the door.

God, We Know How to Go On Without You

Frankly, *I think we have lost our ability to honor God in our churches*. We sing our praise songs with enthusiasm for a little while, but as soon as some of the more radical people in the congregation begin to press into genuine worship, we start glancing at our watches. We might as well say what is in our hearts: "Okay, God, we sure would like it if You would come, but if You don't do it pretty soon, we know how to go on without You. We have a schedule to keep, You know. We can't let First Church beat us to the Me First Diner."

I don't think we realize that His answer is, "Go on. It's okay. Maybe I'll catch up with you some other time." My Bible says that Jesus wept over Jerusalem and her people when they missed their hour of visitation. I wonder if God weeps over us when we grieve His Spirit by clinging to our agendas, schedules, and dinner forks instead of lingering, pursuing, and wooing Him with our worship and adoration? *(Who will be held responsible for causing our cities to miss their visitation too?)*

This sad scenario goes on service after service. We go through the motions of religious duty week after week and year after year thinking we have "arrived." The truth is that the machinery of rote religious practice will clank on long after the oil of God's anointing has drained out. *Inevitably, friction is created when men try to function without the oil of gladness that comes only from His presence.* Eventually everything will come grinding to a halt when the religious machine of man seizes up.

When God revealed Himself to young David in the sheep fields, a longing was born in David's heart to have God's presence close to him day and night. The same thing is happening across the globe in our generation. God is raising up millions of God chasers who are being consumed with a longing for God's presence. We all need to learn from King David's experiences as a God chaser. We know he met disaster in his first *David* attempt to return the ark to Jerusalem, but he was successful his second time around. He was able to open the heavens over Jerusalem through sacrificial, sweaty pursuit of God's *shekinah* glory. *Now it is our turn*—and our cities' turn!

Somebody Has to Tend the Fire!

David did two things to make sure God's presence remained in Jerusalem. First, he prepared a place for God's presence by constructing a tabernacle without walls or a veil. Second, he did something special once the Levites arrived at the tabernacle and set the ark of the covenant in place. He created a "living" mercy seat of worship in the tabernacle so God would be pleased to sit and remain in that humble sanctuary.

David learned a vital secret somewhere in the process of bringing God's presence into Jerusalem. He learned that if you want to keep that blue flame there, *somebody has to tend the fire!* "Do you mean we have to throw logs on the fire?" No, you don't fuel that blue flame of God's *shekinah* presence with earthly fuel. You fuel it through sacrificial worship. *We have no right to call for the fire of God unless we are willing to be the fuel of God.*

David was simply following the heavenly pattern Moses had received for the mercy seat:

> *And you shall make two cherubim of gold; of* **hammered** *work you shall make them at the two ends of the mercy seat. Make one cherub at one end, and the other cherub at the other end; you shall make the cherubim at the two ends of it of one piece with the mercy seat. And the cherubim shall stretch out their wings above, covering the mercy seat with their wings, and they shall face one another; the faces of the cherubim shall be toward the mercy seat.*[2]

The wings of the cherubim that Moses built touched each other as they encircled and covered the mercy seat where the presence of God would sit just above the lid or "covering." If you read this passage closely, you will notice that the two golden cherubim weren't cast or poured into molds. God said that the gold used to form the covering cherubim had to be "beaten" into the proper shape and position.

The way we can build a mercy seat is to take our positions as purified, "beaten" worshipers. One problem is that God still requires mercy seat worshipers to be formed of gold tried in the fire (purified), conformed (beaten) into the image of perfection, and moved into the proper position of unity for worship.[3] This speaks of purity, brokenness, and unity—the three components of true worship under the new covenant of the blood of Jesus. *Brokenness on the earth creates openness in the heavens.*

It is interesting to me that when gold is refined over extreme heat, the first things to come to the top and be skimmed off are the "dross," the obvious impurities and foreign matter. The last thing to be separated from gold is silver, a lesser precious metal that often blends with the raw gold ore. *We often have a hard time separating the "good" from the "best."*

The Hammer Blows of Life
Will Bend Us Godward If...

Too many of us just want to be pre-formed or pre-cast in a quick and easy "one-two-three revival formula." I can't give that to you. However, I can tell you that your wings of worship can be created only one way. They must be beaten into the proper position and the proper image. *The hammer blows of life will bend us "Godward" if our responses to life's challenges are right.* Sometimes we respond wrongly to what life sends us; then the adversity beats us out of position. *Instead of becoming "better" we become "bitter."* This means that our wings of worship will not be where they are supposed to be; they will be in the right place but in the wrong position—in church but with a wrong attitude.

God intends for the hammer blows of life to move your wings of worship into position so as to create one who "in all things gives thanks."[4] The apostle Paul knew about this. He wrote, "For to me to live is Christ, and to die is gain."[5] He wrote these words while under Roman house arrest and awaiting the verdict of Caesar. Paul could declare, "Every time you hit me, all it does is teach me how to worship!" *His visit to the third heaven came while being stoned at Lystra!* Anybody want to go there now?

When the worshipers around the mercy seat come into *their* position, God can move into *His* position and occupy the middle ground between them.

The beaten gold cherubim of the ark of the covenant were only a poor earthly representation of the heavenly reality. Moses saw the pattern on the mount when he peeked into Heaven and saw the throne room in a vision. He was instructed to recreate that heavenly vision, and it is as if the closest he could come on earth was to create solid gold cherubim that only had two wings. The seraphim surrounding God's true heavenly throne have six wings.

The mercy seat on the ark was only a representation of God's true throne in the third heaven. The throne in the heavenlies isn't situated on a two-dimensional plane, so it can't be described solely with width and height measurements. The ark of the covenant featured two cherubim mounted on the flat cover of the ark. In contrast, the Scriptures describe the true throne of God as multidimensional and surrounded by worshipers on all sides, much like a pearl suspended in glass or the sun in the middle of our solar system. The Bible says there are six-winged seraphim on both sides of the throne and more above and beneath as well. These worshiping seraphim cover their faces with two wings while covering their feet with two more wings, and flying with the third pair.[6]

Even though the cherubim on the ark amounted to a "cheap earthly imitation" of the heavenly reality, there is still so much mystique about the ark that Hollywood producers made millions of dollars simply by talking about the "lost ark" in an adventure film.

When will the Church realize that God isn't looking for the lost ark; He knows where that is. *He is looking for "the lost worshipers"* so He can replace the lost glory in the earth.

The Sudden Weight of His Coming Rocked the Earth

The "mercy seat" rarely if ever appears in the midst of religious pomp and circumstance. Under the covenant of Christ's blood, it only comes between two or more living sacrifices. Paul and Silas were far from the ornate temple and the synagogues of Jerusalem and Israel; they were bloodied and battered with their feet locked in stocks deep in a Philippian jail cell. Yet at their darkest hour, these men began to pray and sing to the Lord in worship and adoration. All they did was bring together their battered wings of worship and the glory of God descended from Heaven to join them there. Their worship created the "mercy seat" for God to come and sit between them—*even in jail.*

You may be "in jail" even as you read these words. the circumstances of life have locked you up and thro the key. There is a way of escape. *"Worship" a hole in the heavenlies.* God will come down. He promised. What He did for Paul and Silas He will do for you.

The sudden weight of His coming rocked the earth and shook the foundations of their prison. Not only did the weight of God's presence free His worshipers, but it also opened every door and freed every prisoner in the vicinity! *Our worship can set captives free.* God's visitation in power led to the salvation of the same jailer who had put the stocks on the feet of Paul and Silas.

Don't fear adversity! The cherubim were formed of beaten gold. And worshipers formed of fire-purified gold and beaten through adversity and trials in our day, refract the light of God's glory in the house a lot better than quickie pre-cast versions. Every hammer indentation, every pick and awl mark, and every crease of transformation under pressure of pounding is another reflector for the multifaceted glory of God.

When we worship in spirit and in truth, the glory of God will come. What we will experience at that point is simply a precursor of what will happen on that great day when the King of Glory personally returns to the earth for the second time. The first time He came, He carried His glory lightly because He walked in humility. He tiptoed through our world so He would not disturb His creation, much as an adult tiptoes through a child's playroom to avoid breaking the toys.

The next time Jesus appears, He will be astride a horse and will come in unrestrained power and authority to repossess the entire house. When His feet touch the top of the Mount of Olives, His *kabod*, His weighty glory, will be so great that the Mount of Olives will literally split in two. The eastern gate will suddenly open to allow His "real" triumphant entry. *The first was just the rehearsal. **Next time He will be in costume!*** And every knee will bow and every tongue will confess that Jesus Christ is Lord.[7]

Every Unholy Thing Will Be Leveled Under the Weight of His Glory

Do you know what will break open the gate of your city? Do you know how to split apart the mountains that block your way to revival? Just do what Paul and Silas did in prison. If you can sing at midnight with your back beaten, your feet in stocks, and your cell door locked, then you can usher in the manifested presence and glory of God through your worship. Every unholy thing will be leveled and every bond will fall away under the weight of His glory: "Suddenly there was a great earthquake, so that the foundations of the prison were shaken; and immediately all the doors were opened and everyone's chains were loosed."[8]

All this happens *when the beaten wings of worshipers touch, creating the mercy seat* of God. The New American Version of Psalm 22:3 says God is "enthroned upon the praises of Israel." I am told that the Japanese translation of the original Hebrew text for this verse literally says that our praise *"builds a big chair for God to sit on."* Jesus also told us, "For where two or three are gathered together in My name, there am I in the *midst* of them."[9] That means God comes to dwell in the "middle" of us when we begin to worship Him together.

What would happen if God literally moved His throne from Heaven to sit in the "big chair" we have built for Him? I think He might say, "Michael, Gabriel, I'll see you. The sons of Adam built a chair for Me. They built a living mercy seat just for Me so I can once again dwell among men."

David Fueled the Flame of God's Presence With 24-Hour Worship

How can we recreate or "compete" with the kind of worship God receives in Heaven? David instructed sanctified Levites to keep fueling the flame of God's presence with 24-hour worship every day. (Don't get into legalism and think, "I have to help my church set up a 24-hour prayer vigil." If God tells you and your church leadership to do it, then do it. If not, ask Him what He wants you to do and do it.)

Remember that you can beg for God to come all you want, but until you prepare a place where His weighty glory can safely dwell, He may visit but He cannot stay. I don't know about you, but I am tired of visits. Somehow we have to reclaim the ability to *host the Holy Ghost*. David knew how to do it.

David surrounded that ark with worshipers so that the glory of God would keep flickering. For the first time in history, Israelites, pagans, or heathen could stand near Mount Zion in Jerusalem and literally see the blue flame of God's glory flickering between the outstretched arms and dancing feet of the worshipers in David's tabernacle! How could this be? It was because David's tabernacle was a place marked by open-veiled and unfettered worship.

I often illustrate this concept of surrounding God with worship in public meetings by calling up three or more volunteers to join me in front of the audience or congregation. Almost every time one of the volunteers will step into position facing the audience because that is the way we have been conditioned. I'll tell the volunteer (for the benefit of the audience), "No, son, don't face the congregation or the choir. Stand right here and lift up your hands in a posture of worship toward the One on the throne."

(This may explain why the world can't see God when it looks at the Church—it sees only us. That is probably because we don't stand in the gap, and we prefer to face the world instead of God while performing our religious duties. There is too much of man in the church, and too little of God.) Facing man can only cause us to respond to man's approval. *For "mercy seat" worship, you must turn your back on man.* **Seek the face of God. Lose the fear of man—and gain the fear of God.**

This Is the Miracle of God's Favorite House

David did more than surround the ark of God with sanctified worshipers. He made sure that their primary focus was to minister to God through praise, worship, and adoration. The Levites, the Old Testament ministers of worship and praise, stood between the world on the outside and the unveiled glory of God on the inside.

For the first time since His final walk with Adam and Eve in the garden of Eden, God found a house where there was no veil or dividing walls between His glory and the frail flesh of men. It wasn't needed because *the worshipers had become the veil* and protective walls as they surrounded God's glory with a covering cloud of repentant, sacrificial worship and praise. For lack of a better term, I call this precarious place between the porch of man and the altar of God *"the weeping zone."* This is the miracle that made David's humble tent become God's favorite house.

Two key Scripture passages may help you understand why David managed to build a tabernacle without a veil or walls without seeing people die by the hundreds or thousands. First, God said, "And I sought for a man among them, that should make up the hedge, and stand in the gap before Me for the land, that I should not destroy it: but I found none."[10] Secondly, John seems to describe the two components of God's glory when he wrote, "We beheld His glory...full of grace and truth."[11]

Forget What People Say; Only One Opinion Matters

If you really want an outbreak of the glory of God in your church and city, you will have to forget about what anybody else except God thinks. Real revival happens only when true worshipers forget about man and turn their full attention and adoration toward God. We must forget about the opinions and approval or disapproval of people. We need to forget what they look like, forget what they are saying, and forget what they are thinking. *Only one opinion matters.*

I wish that God's people would ignore everything but what God wants. It is time for the centrality of Christ Jesus to so overwhelm and overpower us that we become totally disconnected from the distractions of the realm of man. I'm not talking about becoming so religious that we are absolutely no good to God or man. Some people say that you can become so heavenly minded that you are no earthly good, but I'm not sure that is possible. In fact, that phrase is a good description of the "weeping zone," that place between the porch of man and the altar of God. Can I tell you what you do in that position? *The weeping zone is the place of intercession before God's throne* where you step into the gap to intercede for others.

Take a Stand Between the Glory and Sinful Men

A plague of sin and death is sweeping across our nation and the world today. This is no time to run or hide. This is the time for you and me to enter the weeping zone with our priestly censers of worship and take our stand between the living and the dead, between the weighty glory of God and the unprotected flesh of sinful men. The moment Aaron carried the coals from the fire of the altar and mixed in the incense of worship and prayer, he became a bridge between two worlds.

God has a heart to see all men saved, but He depends on you and me to fulfill our ministry of reconciliation in the weeping zone. He has called us to become bridges between the kingdom of light and the kingdom of darkness. The greatest Bridge of all is Jesus Christ, our great High Priest who ever lives to intercede for us before the Father.[12] When you and I enter the weeping zone, we come alongside the Great Intercessor and face the throne, reaching out for God with one hand and for man with the other. We are called to intercede in worship until God and man have met together.

When you stand in the gap, you are literally stopping the judgment of God and moving aside the obstacles of the enemy in the second heaven. As we noted earlier, John said, "We beheld His glory...full of grace and truth."[13]

If the two components of God's glory are grace and truth, then that explains why there always had to be a veil separating man from God's glory. *The world needs God's grace, but His truth is attached to it.* The truth is, we have all sinned and come short of the glory of God.[14] We need His grace—but we can't stand the "truth." His truth is equivalent to His *judgment*, and apart from God's grace through Jesus Christ, none of us have a chance. That means that if God's manifest presence—the thing we are praying for—rushes out and encounters unrepentant flesh, then the truth or judgment of God will instantly obliterate it just as light obliterates darkness.

Follow Him to the Weeping Zone for the Lost

Jesus Christ did a finished work on the cross, and He extends the free gift of life to everyone. Our "ministry of reconciliation" involves taking up His cross daily and following Him into the weeping zone for the lost. When repentant, bloody-handed, sacrificing worshipers take their place between the unredeemed and the consuming glory of God, an interesting thing happens.

We know from the Scriptures that judgment begins and ends at the house of God.[15] When God's people become worshipers and stand in the gap, *they "filter" the truth and judgment component of glory.* That means that the only component of God's glory that rushes past them to flow in the streets of the city is grace and mercy. This is reminiscent of David's day, when anyone and everyone could look at the *shekinah* glory of God and live because they were peering at the mercy seat between the covering filter of the outstretched arms of worshipers.

Our cities don't need better sermons or better songs. They need "gap people" who can reach for God with one hand and for the world with the other. Are you called to take a stand in the weeping zone? Can you forget what man says while reaching out to God with one hand in repentant, broken worship and reaching out to unredeemed man with the other? With that hand extended, you declare: "I am going to open the heavens and keep them propped open until revival sweeps through my city!" Like the intercessors of old, we must cry, "If You are going to kill them, then kill me. If You don't send revival to my nation, just kill me. Give me spiritual children, or I die."[16]

Do you really want revival? *Build a mercy seat for God.* Prepare something that is so desirable and attractive to God that He can't resist joining you and the worshipers. Allow Him to build again the tabernacle of David in your midst. Surround Him with worship and adoration if you want to entice Him to come and stay with you. *Build a mercy seat!*

God Dwells in the *Middle* of Worship

Can you imagine what would happen if He left His throne in Heaven to come sit with us in a mercy seat composed of our praise and worship? There is a reason the world can't see Him as He is. *We have never built a place for Him to sit.* Foxes have holes and birds have nests, but the glory of God has no place to sit—no earthly mercy seat! Of course our furniture is simple by Heaven's standards, and we could never pass for six-winged seraphim. How can earthly worship match heavenly worship? I don't know, but I do know it doesn't take much! Jesus said, "If I can just get two or three of you to agree, I'll come in—not to the side, but in the middle of them."[17] Why? Because God dwells in the middle of the worship.

If you want the manifested presence of God to break out in your church and city, then remember that He probably won't come to me alone, nor to you alone. His first choice and His promise is that He will come *in the middle* of us as we worship Him according to the heavenly pattern.

If you build it, He will come!

"Father, You said that out of the mouth of babes and sucklings You have perfected praise. We admit that our best is pitiful praise, that it cannot match the heavenly vision, that it cannot reach the heights of perfection we understand is in Heaven.

"Nevertheless, according to the heavenly pattern, we delight in surrounding You with repentant worship. Rebuild Your beloved tabernacle of David in our hearts, dear Lord. Yes, we will

worship You with all our hearts. Yes, with joy we will bow down before You as our Lord and King.

"We call for Your manifested presence to fill this place, Father. We ask You to fill this city, to fill this nation, to fill this world until the whole earth is covered with Your glory, O God, like the waters cover the sea. Come sit in our midst on Your mercy seat!"

Endnotes

1. James Strong, *Strong's Exhaustive Concordance of the Bible* (Peabody, MA: Hendrickson Publishers, n.d.), **glory** (#H3519, #H3513).
2. Exodus 25:18-20 NKJV.
3. See Revelation 3:18; Romans 8:29.
4. See 1 Thessalonians 5:18.
5. Philippians 1:21.
6. See Isaiah 6:2.
7. See Philippians 2:10-11.
8. Acts 16:26 NKJV.
9. Matthew 18:20.
10. Ezekiel 22:30.
11. John 1:14b.
12. See Hebrews 7:25.
13. John 1:14b.
14. See Romans 3:23.
15. See 1 Peter 4:17.
16. See Exodus 32; Genesis 30:1.
17. See Matthew 18:20.

Chapter 5

Turning on the Light of His Glory
No More Stumbling in the Dark

How do you turn on the light of the glory of God? If you were raised in an older house or if you ever visited Grandma's house where the old-fashioned light fixtures had pull strings hanging from the ceiling, you will understand what I am about to say.

Do you remember what it was like trying to find that little pull string in the dark? There were no wall switches conveniently located beside the door. If you wanted to turn on the light in the middle of the night, there was only one way to do it. You had to "wade into the darkness" blindly waving your hands in the general direction of the pull string. Perhaps you have even barked your shin or stubbed your toe on furniture while stumbling around in the dark trying to find that string.

If we could somehow capture on videotape some of the crazy things people do when they are trying to find pull-string light switches, it would be hilarious. People on the hunt for pull-string light switches often wave their arms like madmen. They jump in desperation; they crouch down, halfway expecting a painful meeting with the shin-cracking edge of the coffee table. The more cautious ones reach up with one hand over their head and wave it back and forth....

The same thing happens in our churches sometimes. People who come in for the first time and see us going through some odd antics in our services ask, "What in the world are you doing?" All we can tell them is, "*We're hunting for the light switch.* If we can ever turn on the light of the glory of God in this place, you will understand." We may stumble around and wave our arms aimlessly for a time while we search for the light switch, but we know that the preexistent light of God's glory means everything! If we can just turn on the light of His glory, then suddenly everyone will see and know the difference between truth and error. Most people will choose truth when given the opportunity; it is just that *they have never have had enough light around them to see the way.* The light of God's glory existed before the sun and moon, and it will continue to exist after they have been snuffed out. Somehow it must be made manifest!

Once we find out how to turn on the light of God's glory, we can determine how to *keep* that spiritual light shining. *This is what I call an open heaven!* We must keep the heavens open over that place of easy access to God's presence. When you live under an open heaven, the same altar call that used to bring two people to the Lord will inexplicably bring 200 running forward to receive Christ. That is comparable to the difference between sawing lumber with a handsaw and doing the same job with a power saw. For generations, we have struggled to free the lost from satan's bondage using the anointing. God has opened the door for us to do it much quicker and easier through the revelation of *His glory* in our lives and churches. The anointing can quickly draw a crowd, and it can easily affect a crowd. However, when God comes down and reveals His glory among us, the entire city will be affected!

The ministry of Charles G. Finney was marked by city-transforming revivals. The city of Utica, New York, was dramatically changed by the power of God resident in the life of

Finney, a man who burned with the passion of deep prayer and an intimate relationship with God.

It is said that when Finney walked through the knitting mills of Utica in the late 1800's, the presence of God was so strong that workers began to fall to their knees in repentance even before he opened his mouth! Ultimately, the entire city and region were affected because of the presence of God he carried with him. *It was as if he carried a light with him that suddenly allowed men to view themselves and God from a right perspective.* When the Presence came near, men knew that they were dirty and that God was holy! This seems to be a modern-day fulfillment of Isaiah's prophecy:

> *Arise, shine; for your light has come! And the glory of the Lord is risen upon you. For behold, the darkness shall cover the earth, and deep darkness the people; but the Lord will arise over you, and His glory will be seen upon you. The Gentiles shall come to your light, and kings to the brightness of your rising.*[1]

While ministering in that city, I asked my host to take me to the same mills Finney visited so many years before. The mills were abandoned long ago, and the people who worked there and experienced the power of God are gone now. Even so, the potential of God still seems to linger in the silence of those buildings. I leaned against the wall of one of the mills and just wept as I prayed, "God, I want to be a person who props open the windows of Heaven so much that people will have an encounter with You just by being around me."

The People in Darkness Have Seen a Great Light

When someone pays the price to open the windows of Heaven through sacrificial, repentant worship, the light of God's manifested presence beams across the dreary landscape of human souls and lets everybody know that it's time to be free. This is what the prophet Isaiah meant when he prophesied of Christ's coming: "The people who walked in darkness have seen a great light; those who dwelt in the land of the shadow of death, upon them a light has shined."[2]

You know that you have encountered the pure presence of God as a result of an open heaven when people who live in "the land of the shadow of death" see a great light. *This is the manifested presence of God.* When the heavens open over a city or nation, there is a heightened sense of the presence of God on the earth. This is the ultimate form of "spiritual warfare."

I am convinced that most of our so-called spiritual warfare amounts to nothing but a bunch of kids threatening to call their Daddy. The enemy always has been able to tell the difference between the real thing and the "wannabes." The seven sons of Sceva in the Book of Acts thought that they could use the same weapon they saw Paul using against demons. All it got them was a severe beating and enough embarrassment to last a lifetime.[3]

Satan and his imps are like bullying dogs. They can sense when someone is afraid of them, even when the person is yelling and waving a weapon. They also know who *isn't* afraid of them and avoid direct conflict with them. Perhaps this has to do with whether or not God is really our Father. For spiritual warfare to be effective, you must stand firmly on the ground of relationship.

God's Presence Disarms the Forces of Darkness

There is a theology of God's presence. When His manifested presence appears in any area or vicinity, the forces of darkness lose their ability to sway the public (again, this is His concentrated manifest presence as opposed to His omnipresence). As I wrote in *The God Chasers,*

> "When the sole of Jesus' foot touched the sandy shore of Gadara, one half-mile distant a man possessed of 5,000 demons suddenly was freed from their choking grasp for the first time....

> "We need to hear the footfall of God as the sole of His foot touches earth just one time.... When that happens, we won't have to worry about telling little demons to run."[4]

The reason you should desire an open heaven over your church and city is because the demonic forces whom we battle lose their authority in the manifest presence of God.[5] When God comes on the scene, there simply *isn't* a battle! There is no one left standing to even think about challenging Him. Even the demons are too busy running away or bowing their knee to the Almighty One. That is why I so emphasize the importance of opening the windows of Heaven by creating an environment where the manifest presence of God is pleased to dwell.

The World Doesn't Fear Him Because the Church Doesn't Fear Him

The manifest presence of God brings people from every walk of life to a place where they fear the name of the Lord. *The reason that the world doesn't really fear God is because most of us in the Church don't really fear Him either.* For many years, Christianity, for the most part, has been absent of a visitation of the fear of God. How could they fear Him whose power they have never experienced? We like to talk about it while never really understanding it! But if you ever experience it, you will understand. *Just as an encounter with electricity leaves you with a permanently endowed memory, so does a legitimate encounter with the manifest presence of God.* I think God's version of spiritual warfare is totally different from ours. Isaiah described it this way:

> *So shall they fear the name of the Lord from the west, and His glory from the rising of the sun. When the enemy shall come in like a flood, the Spirit of the Lord shall lift up a standard against him.*[6]

The Hebrew language has no punctuation marks—especially the ancient Hebrew used in the oldest manuscripts. The translators in King James' day did the best they could, but modern translators brought new scholarship and understanding of the original languages to this passage.

To understand the reading favored by most modern scholars, just move the comma so the passage reads this way: "When the enemy shall come in, ***like a flood*** *the Spirit of the Lord shall lift up a standard against him.*" The New International Version says, "From the west, men will fear the name of the Lord, and from the rising of the sun, they will revere His glory. For He will come like a pent-up flood that the breath of the Lord drives along."[7] The total focus of the passage is on the coming of the glory or the manifest presence of God.

Revival Is an Outright Invasion of Satan's Kingdom

The prophet's message continues right on through our modern chapter divisions to where Isaiah prophesies, "Arise, shine; for your light has come! And the glory of the Lord is risen upon you. For behold, the darkness shall cover the earth, and deep darkness the people; but the Lord will arise over you, and His glory will be seen upon you."[8] This is what I mean when I talk about "turning on the light of His presence."

Since revival is essentially an outright invasion and overthrow of satan's kingdom in the earth, it is appropriate for the topic of spiritual warfare to come up. There is a place for Bible-based, Spirit-led binding and loosing by the saints, but most of the time we concentrate on the binding. We also tend to go at it like scared kids trapped inside a fence with a mean junkyard dog. We bind the devil, we bind the demons, we bind the weather clouds, we bind the neighbor's noisy dog and the ornery neighbor himself, and we may even try to bind the fouled spark plug that causes the car engine to miss. Never mind that you never mentioned the engine! In other words, we tend to go way too far over the line of reason and reasonableness.

We should *loose something in the heavenly realm* every time we feel led to bind something on earth. Never pray to bind the devil unless you also pray to loose the power of Jesus and the Spirit of God in that situation. *If you bind one thing and don't loose something else, you really haven't done anything but tie everything up in knots.* **Whenever I pray that God would "open the windows of Heaven," I also pray that He would close "the gates of hell!"**

When Jesus said "the gates of hell shall not prevail," He meant that they don't have authority over the redeemed or God's Kingdom.[9] When the gates of Heaven open, it is time to storm the enemy's gates and *plunder hell to populate Heaven*. It helps us to know that satan no longer has possession of the "keys to hell." Jesus recovered them! *Satan can't even lock the doors to his own house!*

Let's Set the Record Straight About the "Great Celestial Conflict"

Sometimes we hear preachers wax poetic with grand descriptions of the "celestial conflict" in Heaven when the archangel lucifer was cast out of God's presence and fell to the earth. It is true that lucifer was cast out of Heaven along with a third of the angels. However, *there was no big fight in Heaven*.[10]

The apostle John wrote, "God is light, and in Him is no darkness at all."[11] God can discern the difference between a thought and an intent[12] (but no one else can). When something moves from being a thought to becoming an intent, it becomes sin before you ever commit the actual deed. That is why Jesus said that if a man looked on a woman to lust after her, he had crossed the line.[13]

Lucifer was an archangel in charge of the worship in the heavenly realm. The *thought* entered his mind that he would rise up to supersede God, who is the origin of all things. What a silly thought! He should have dismissed it immediately, but he didn't. When the thought of ascending to the throne of God entered lucifer's mind, there was no problem until he said, "I'm going to try that." The moment it moved from a thought to an intent, the tiniest speck of sin appeared in the bright white light of the glory of God—and it was gone in less than a nanosecond. The "war" was declared over and lucifer, now satan, was cast out of there.

Lucifer didn't gather up a third of the angelic corps and say, "Okay, we're going to go to battle for the whole works. We're taking the Big Guy down today." There was no real war. God

God put satan down by his word & power of authority

didn't get up one day and say, "Michael, Gabriel, you guys need to put your swords on. I'm having a problem with lucifer. He is trying to push Me off My throne and I need your help."

How Long Does It Take Darkness to Flee?

There was no cosmic war in Heaven in which God finally managed to prevail and returned to Heaven saying, "Whooo, that was a tough one." It didn't happen like that. The moment lucifer's thought shifted to the realm of intent, in that immeasurable microsecond a tiny speck of darkness appeared in the heavenly realm, He who is Light cast out that darkness instantly. *How long does it take for darkness to flee the room when you flip on the light switch?* There is no battle between photons of light and subatomic particles of darkness. No, when the light comes on, the darkness is obliterated faster than the blink of an eye. That is why Jesus said, "I beheld Satan as lightning fall from heaven."[14]

In less than a split second, lucifer was stripped of his name, position, and heavenly office, and thrown out of the heavenly glory-filled realm at the speed of light. He barely managed to stay one step ahead of that light as he was cast down, and then darkness fell on the face of the deep.

Satan thought that he had found a place of refuge until God leaned over and saw that the world He had created in absolute beauty had become a place of chaos, void and without form. God corrected that problem by decreeing, "Let there be light." The glory of God fell upon the earth and there was light from the emanation of His own presence—even before He created the sun![15]

My friend, we face very similar circumstances today: Darkness once again covers the face of the deep. It is interesting to note that the darkness affects only the surface or the "face." *Satan is occupying; he doesn't own.* He is just camping out here because he can't go to the depths of the thing. He's covering all the territory that he can, but his darkness only covers the face of things. His influence is wide, but his strength is shallow!

darkness = face of the Earth (of things) surface

Turning on the Light of His Glory

I remember the time I stood side by side with other believers and looked out over the city of Los Angeles. We prayed and I stretched my hand out toward the valley that is home to about 15 million people. On the face of it, things look pretty dark in that vast city, but it isn't very deep. If you scratch the surface, you will find hungry-hearted people who are just waiting for a flicker of light to come to them. It is that way in your city also! *If worship can ever scratch the surface, the hungry will find you!* They will follow the "light" to its source, just as the wise men of old followed the heavenly light to Christ. Worship opens a window—a window for God's glory to stream down. Humanity is then drawn to the light.

"O God—where is that light switch?! Where is that window?"

It is our job to intercede to the King for the people who dwell in darkness. Like Queen Esther who interceded for the life of her people, we must be willing to pay any price to see God's glory shine upon our churches and cities. *That brings up God's problem.* Sin can't stand in His presence because He is light, and there is no darkness in Him—none at all. Yet He longs to walk with you and me in the cool of the morning as He did with Adam and Eve before they fell into sin.

This Is What Glory Does to the Flesh of Man

We all can agree that Jesus Christ shed His blood to take care of this sin problem. Yet in every instance where I have seen a measure of God's glory enter a worship service, *a godly reverence, fear, and dread of His glory also entered the room.* Even redeemed, blood-washed church leaders who lead holy lives suddenly feel a deep urgency to fall on their faces and repent before their holy God when His *kabod,* or weighty presence, begins to fill the room. This is what glory does to the flesh of man—even the flesh of the redeemed. This is why the earthy disciples always had to be reassured when a theophany or an angel appeared before them. *They feared that the glory would kill them!*

For this reason, God says to us with one hand, "Come close." Yet with the other hand He says, "Not so fast." It can be frightening to come too close to God's holy presence when there are specks of unrepented sin in your life. Yes, we are covered by the blood of Christ, but that doesn't release us from the felt need to repent of our sins and shortcomings anew when we encounter the holiness of His presence. Do we need to "get saved all over again"? Absolutely not! But do we often *feel* like "getting saved all over again"? Absolutely! Isaiah did! John did—he fell at His feet "as though dead"![16]

Jesus covers us with His blood to allow us to come into His presence in our unregenerated state. "What do you mean, unregenerated?" We are not perfect, but we are living under the mantle of forgiveness—we are covered by the blood of the perfect sinless sacrifice—so we can enter in. That is where we're at now under the new covenant of Christ's blood, but somehow David stumbled across that same principle under the old covenants of Moses and the Old Testament when he began transporting the ark from Obededom's house. *It was a bloody, smoky process that led to David's wild dance through the gates of Jerusalem.*

What we are learning from his experience is that the repentant, brokenhearted nature of true worship only heightens the rich aroma of our acceptable sacrifice to God, and it is this offering that persuades the King of Glory to habitate with us instead of merely visit our meetings.[17] When His glory finally comes through the gates of worship into our churches and cities, *we too might become dancing fools!*

There is no better way to wage spiritual warfare than to turn on the light of God's glory by ushering in His manifest presence. Allow Him to rebuild His favorite house in your gatherings and refuse to stop short at false finish lines or to be satisfied merely by the scent of where He once was.

Persist in your urgent longing for and pursuit of His presence and the heavens will open; His *shekinah* glory will descend on the mercy seat that your love and adoration have made just for Him. It is in this atmosphere of intimacy and devotion to God and God alone where His manifest presence shows up.

Decimated =

When He turns on the light of His glory, demonic forces are instantly decimated. Captives are released and set free to run to their **Redeemer** just as the demoniac was released even before he met or heard Jesus speak.

When the heavens are open and God's light shines on the darkness, every demon and dark work is forced out because *the gates of hell can never prevail* or even put up a respectable fight when the very presence of the King of glory shows up. *Conduct spiritual warfare for your church and city in the same way God conducts it in Heaven* and you'll create a "DFZ" (a demon-free zone)! Pray and worship Him until the windows of Heaven open wide over your church and city. Worship Him until the light of His glory shines upon you. *Demon Free Zone*

"O Lord, on earth as it is in Heaven—show us Your glory!"

Endnotes

Way God conducks warfare in heaven. D.F.Z. demon free zone

1. Isaiah 60:1-3 NKJV.
2. Isaiah 9:2 NKJV.
3. See Acts 19:14-17.
4. Tommy Tenney, *The God Chasers* (Shippensburg, PA: Destiny Image Publishers, 1998), 114-115.
5. See the confrontation between Jesus and the demoniac in Mark 5:2-6.
6. Isaiah 59:19.
7. Isaiah 59:19 NIV.
8. Isaiah 60:1-2 NKJV.
9. Matthew 16:18.
10. See Isaiah 14:12-15; Luke 10:18.
11. 1 John 1:5b.
12. See Hebrews 4:12.
13. See Matthew 5:28.
14. Luke 10:18.
15. God declared, "Let there be light" on the *first* day of creation (see Gen. 1:3-5). The Bible says that the sun and the other lesser lights weren't created until the *fourth* day (see Gen. 1:14-19).

4th day of creation

16.   See Revelation 1:17. Perhaps this same apostle put it best in his letter to fellow Christians: "If we confess our sins, He is faithful and just to forgive us our sins, and to cleanse us from all unrighteousness" (1 Jn. 1:9).

17.   Once again, let me clearly note that this concept of "habitation" refers to the concentrated glory or manifested presence of God (referred to as His *kabod* or "weighty glory"). It should be understood that the Holy Spirit dwells continually in the hearts of everyone who repents and receives Jesus Christ as Lord and Savior. This relationship with God cannot be bought, earned, or "worked up" by any form of good works on our part—it is a free gift from God. However, Jesus clearly implied to John that He was "knocking on the hearts" of *believers* in Revelation 3:20, and that He would come and "sup" or feast with them if they *opened the door*. I believe that Jesus is knocking on the door of the Church today. If we respond with desire and actively seek to *open the door of Heaven*, He will come and feast with us in His *shekinah* glory.

Chapter 6

Never Trust Anyone Without a Limp
Wrestling With Divine Destiny

G od's people need more than just another "good meeting" that sends goose bumps up and down their spines. *We need a God-meeting that leaves us with a limp!* Where are the Jacobs who will lay hold on the theophany of God and wrestle with their destiny until it is changed? Who will take hold of God and say, "I am not going to let go until You bless me"?

> *Then Jacob was left alone; and a Man wrestled with him until the breaking of day. Now when He saw that He did not prevail against him, He touched the socket of his hip; and **the socket of Jacob's hip was out of joint as He wrestled** with him. And He said, "Let Me go, for the day breaks." But he said, "**I will not let You go unless You bless me!**"*[1]

Many people wonder how Jacob could use such improper, impertinent language with God Almighty. I believe that Jacob, "the heel-grabber," used the only terminology he understood. He may have become a patriarch, but he wasn't a theologian.

...e of passion will desperately pursue what the educated tell them ...n't be caught. Jacob knew what a blessing was because he remembered what happened when his father laid his hand on his head:

> "All I know is that my father's blessing changed my life and made things different, and I've got to have something like that again. The only thing I know to call it is a 'blessing,' so touch me.

> "I've got to have it. I've already had a blessing from the earthly perspective. Now I need it from a heavenly perspective. I am not going to let You go until You bless me."

This Isn't Some Celestial "Blue-Light Special"

All too often we approach God with a discount store mentality. Whether we come for revival, physical healing, or a financial blessing, we hope to get what we want at the cheapest price in the shortest time possible. I don't know about you, but I have never seen God do things that way. We like to line up like we've found some celestial "blue-light special" with our lists of prayers and petitions. Then we say, "Bless me." I have begun to pray that God would not answer our exact requests, but answer according to our need instead. We know what we want—*but do we know what we need?*

Jacob's name literally means "supplanter" or trickster. He was a lifelong deceiver, a trickster who stole his older brother's birthright and his father's blessing. To say he was untrustworthy was probably an understatement. Yet Jacob came from a good family, the son of one of the most famous men in history. He grew up "in church" because Abraham and Isaac had passed down to their sons the stories of their encounters with God. Jacob had a calling on his life and a divine destiny to fulfill—*but he couldn't be trusted* in his present state. All that was about to change with one encounter.

> So ▓▓▓▓▓▓▓ *What is your name?" He said, "Jacob." And He said, ▓▓▓▓▓▓ be called Jacob, but Israel; **for you have strugg**▓▓▓▓▓▓***th men, and have prevailed.*** *Then Jacob ask*▓▓▓▓*l me Your name, I pray." And He said, "Why is it that you ask about My name?"* **And He blessed him there.** *And Jacob called the name of the place Peniel: "For I have seen God face to face, and my life is preserved."*[2]

After one or two hours of wrestling and grappling for the advantage, Jacob probably felt pretty confident that he was going to receive a blessing. I believe he thought to himself, *Well, at some point this angelic whatever I'm wrestling with, this manifestation of God, is going to say, "Okay, okay, I'll bless you. Now kneel down right here and I'll put my hands on your head."* There was a surprise in store for him.

Don't Bless My Messed-Up Life; Give Me a New Life

The Lord didn't stretch out His arm with an open hand of blessing because Jacob didn't need another blessing on his messed-up life.[3] He needed a new life. Instead, the Lord doubled up His fist and struck Jacob in the thigh with such power that it knocked Jacob's thigh out of joint and permanently injured the connective ligament there. As a result, *Jacob limped the rest of his life.*

When Jacob's older brother, Esau, finally saw Jacob limp into view, he probably thought, *That's not the same Jacob who stole my birthright. He doesn't even walk the same. There is humility in his walk; there is a new tenderness in him. He is different. I can't kill him; that's my brother."* He wanted to kill the *old* brother, but he embraced the *new* Jacob. If we will embrace repentant flesh-death, those who once hated us may see a new version of us.

Jacob probably wanted a blessing that would make his angry older brother submissive to him, but God blessed him in a different way. He *changed* him so that his brother would like him. *It is time for the Church to change too.*

The Church has been strutting down the sidewalks of the world in arrogance, pointing fingers of incrimination in every direction and telling everybody else to "get right." Meanwhile, we have a proverbial board sticking out of our eye that is a mile long. It is time for us to say, "God, I don't know whether You will bring a *blessing* or a *changing*, but something has to happen. Teach us how to build mercy seats instead of judgment seats."

I'm Tired of Getting Touched But Not Changed

We need to have encounters with God that leave us changed forever. *I am tired of coming to church and getting touched but not changed.* We must lock onto the presence of God and say, "I'm not letting You go until something happens inside me and I am never the same again."

This is the God-kind-of-change that permanently wounds the old man and the old ways of doing things. It causes the death of something within us, which marks a change for the better. People should see us coming with a new limp, a new *tenderness borne of the day we lost our wrestling contest with God*. It should make people say, "I like that person. He isn't speaking from a place of pompous arrogance; he speaks like he knows what it's like to come from the bottom." That is why my motto is, *"Never trust anybody who doesn't walk with a limp."*

Every Revivalist Has Wrestled

Duncan Campbell of Hebrides revival fame knew what it was like to "wrestle with destiny and lose." He said,

> "I'll tell you how the Hebrides revival started. It did not really start with me showing up to preach some big conference. It started in my study. Years before, I had been a part of what they called the Faith Mission Movement in England. Before I was married, I rode my bicycle all over England spreading the gospel, preaching, and functioning as best as I knew how, and those were the beginning great days. Those were the seed beds of everything that I eventually became. In the process of that, I decided to go back to school and further my education. I came out at

the top of the dean's list and I began to be known as the Right Reverend Duncan Campbell."[4]

...preacher in England...

going on today, although it is not as large as it once... the best and the brightest were invited to speak at Keswick Week, and the Right Reverend Duncan Campbell was the keynote speaker for this conference year after year. Then *a chance comment by his teenage daughter launched him into a contest with God* that changed his ministry—and the Hebrides Islands—forever.

Why Doesn't God Use You Like He Used To?

Duncan Campbell was in his mid-40s and had entered what he thought was his prime. He was working in his study preparing sermons for yet another Keswick Week appearance when his 15-year-old daughter came in to see him. Daughters are known for their ability to speak the truth without really knowing the impact of what they are saying. (*Most of the things I learned from God, I personally learned through my little girls!*) As Duncan Campbell and his daughter talked, she asked this question: "Dad, why doesn't God use you like He used to?"

Campbell told an English friend of mine,[5] "It knocked the wind out of my sails because I thought I was at the peak. When she asked me that question, I was preparing sermons that would affect all of England, or so I thought. So I put my pen down and asked her, 'My dear, what is it that you mean?' She said, 'Dad, you've told me the stories of what used to happen when you worked in the Faith Mission Movement. Why doesn't God do that with you anymore?' "

"I made some lame brain excuses and tried to theologically talk through it so I wouldn't lose face in front of my daughter," he said. "I held my composure...until she left the room. When she did, I fell on my face and said, 'God, *she is right!*' With my face in the carpet, I wept hot tears and said, 'God, if You will give me back what I had, I will do whatever You tell me to do.' Three weeks later I was sitting on the platform at a conference. I had already spoken and was scheduled to speak again. Then God spoke to me and said, 'Get up and go to the Hebrides Islands, to the Isle of Lewis.' "

If You Go, I Will Give It

"I said, 'God, I'm supposed to speak,' and He said just as clearly as I've ever heard anything said, 'Duncan, on the floor of your study you promised Me that you would do whatever I asked you if I would give you back what you had. *If you will go, I will give it.*' "

Duncan Campbell left the platform immediately and leaned over to the conveners to say, "I'm sorry, something has come up. I've got to go." Within three days he was on the Isle of Lewis. When he stepped off the ferryboat and asked for the pastor, the townspeople replied, "There is no pastor. There are only three churches here; two of them are closed and one has some elderly ladies meeting in it with the postman. But if you're looking for a religious man, the postman is the one you'll be looking for."

The postman was the elder in the church who basically held things together and served as an interim pastor. Duncan Campbell found the postman's house and knocked on the door, not knowing what to expect. The postman answered the door and immediately said, "*Oh, Mr. Campbell, you're right on time. We have just enough time for tea before the meeting starts tonight.*" Over tea, he explained, "The ladies and myself, we've been praying, and God spoke and said you were coming. Six weeks ago I printed posters that announced that the meetings would begin tonight." Mr. Campbell told my English friend, "It dawned on me then that God really didn't *need* me. He had already prepared it, but He really *wanted* me."

Duncan Campbell wrestled with God over his destiny, and he rose from his tear-stained carpet a changed man. Only a man with a limp could be trusted with what would later be called "the New Hebrides revival." This revival gave us a glimpse of what could happen if God comes down upon an entire _____ Christ without hearing a single ser-

____ century ago before the days of widely ___. This "non-tongues-speaking, much-heart-breaking" revival swept an entire region and was nothing less than purely miraculous. It began in the brokenhearted prayers of persistent worshipers and was launched in Duncan Campbell's heart *the day he wrestled with God and lost.*

Jacob Left the Match With a Permanent Trophy of His Defeat

When Jacob lost his contest with God, he was transformed from being a man who was out to take care of Number One any way he could into a prince of God's chosen people. He wrestled with God over his destiny and left the match with a permanent trophy of his defeat. It was the match he needed to lose for his own good. He needed a change if he was ever to move on into his God-ordained destiny. *The Church needs a change too.*

If we are going to move to the next level, we must shift our emphasis away from God's hands to His face. I travel so much that I particularly cherish the time I'm home with my children. One time when my youngest daughter was six years old, I came home and she climbed up in my lap in the recliner. I was tired and was reading the paper or watching the news on television, but she was determined to get my attention. She reached up with those chubby little six-year-old fingers and grabbed my face. At that time she still had a little bit of a childish lisp, and she turned my face away from the distraction and said, *"Wook at me, Daddy. Wook at me."*

Then she just smothered me in kisses, and I gave her a hug before trying to go back to my paper. Once again she grabbed my face and said, *"Wook at me, Daddy,"* until she finally got my attention. After 15 minutes of kissing and incredible cuddling from my six-year-old, she finally melted my heart. Children usually want something when they begin to act like that, so I gave her a big hug and asked her, "Andrea, what do you want?" She said, "*Nothing.* I just want you, Daddy."

I loved on her a little more and she just rubbed my face with her little hands and looked up at me with those big brown eyes while she cocked her little head to the side. Then she sealed it all with a smile and the words, "I wuv you, Daddy."

"Come on, what do you want?" I said, thinking that if it went on this long it was something big. Three times I asked her, "What do you want?" Each time she said, "*Nothing, Daddy. I just want you.*" Finally I told Andrea, "Come on, get in the van." We drove into town and I said, "What do you want, baby girl?" Once again she said, "*Nothing, Daddy. I just want you.*"

Then we pulled up in front of a much advertised toy store, and her eyes lit up. By that time my heart was so melted that what I wanted to do was just go in and say, "Okay, baby girl, just tell me *which half of the store* you want. You can have this half or that half, it doesn't matter." I said, "Pick out whatever you want!"

Is There Anybody Here Who Just Wants Me?

Do you know what she got? A little bottle of soap bubbles with the round wand that you blow through to make floating bubbles. Suddenly it became really obvious that she really didn't want anything. *She had just wanted me!* And because she wanted me, I would have given her anything. How often we come to church services to present our petitions, prophesy this, and say that, while God says, "Is there anybody here who just wants Me?"

The highest level of worship is when we push aside His hands and pursue His face! *His face means His favor.* In the biblical days, when people wouldn't turn their face toward you, that meant you were allowed in their presence but did not have their favor. Absalom lived in Jerusalem for two years without seeing his father or being before the king's face.[6] He could live in the city, but he couldn't enter the throne room.

Can you
Have you entered the Throne Room.

Never Trust Anyone Without a Limp

It is possible to live in the Kingdom and not see His face—to enjoy the covenantal protections of the firefighters, the police, and city infrastructure—but not have the favor of the King. For how long has the Church not been pursuing the true favor of God? We've lived in the Kingdom, demanded what's ours, and got it! As the Father fulfilling the selfish request of the prodigal, He gave him his portion, knowing what he was going to do with it. It is an abuse of blessings to take from the Father's *hands* to finance your journey away from the Father's *face*—to elevate *"blessing"* over *"blesser"*!

We must mature to the point that we can say, "It's not His hands," and push His hands aside to seek His face and say, "I'll be a servant" and "I just want to be where you are." Then our worship is no longer self-serving to get something; instead we begin to just give everything to Him. Instead of "bless me," it becomes "bless Him"! We no longer give to get, but we give out of passion! *Be where He God/Christ is.*

There's a shift coming, and to those kinds of passionate people, He will give the ring of authority and the robe of blessing. He knows now that they won't squander their relationship by pursing His hand instead of His face. God is also determined to change the way we "have church." *Presence over presents!* He longs for the worshiper who will go after the "Giver" more than the "gifts"! Are you that person? Are you a restorer of God's favorite house?

Daddy, You Can Sit Anywhere You Want

One time I was away from home when I called to talk to my youngest daughter, Andrea. I said, "What are you doing, baby girl?" She said, "I'm playing tea party, Daddy." I told her, "Set a place for me right now, and we'll just pretend that I'm there and we'll have tea." "I already did," she replied. "Well, where am I sitting?" I asked, and she said, "Well, I didn't know, so I set five places for you." That melted my heart!

How long has it been since the Church was so desperate for Him that we just said, "Father, You can sit anywhere You want.

Here, there, it doesn't matter. Just come." I answered my daughter, "When I get home, Daddy is going to play tea party with you."

All this took place in the middle of the summer in Louisiana when the temperature hits 95 degrees in the shade with 95 percent humidity. Andrea's little plastic playhouse was in the backyard, right in the hot sun. The minute I walked in the door with suitcases in hand, Andrea was saying, "Come on, Daddy." I hadn't even unpacked, but I had a promise to keep. *It was time for Daddy to go play tea party.*

Her playhouse was so small I'm not sure whether I got in it or put it on! My head was holding up the roof while I sat on the ground. I was barely crammed in Andrea's little playhouse before she had handed me a tiny apron with the command, "Put it on." She had the table set and waiting for me, and we started drinking our imaginary tea. She picked up one cup and said, "Here, Daddy." Then she went around the table, "Here, dolly, and this is for me." Then we sat and "supped" together. Andrea asked me, "Is it good?"

"Oh yes, it's good," I told her, even though we were sweating bullets in the hot sun, sipping imaginary tea. Then Andrea said, "Here, have some cookies." (*They were imaginary cookies.*) Once again, she asked, "Is this fun?" The truth of the matter was that I was miserable, but I was with her, and therefore it was fun. So I said, "Yes, baby, it's fun."

Finally Andrea said, "Daddy, it's hot and I'm thirsty. Let's go in the big house and get something to drink." I said, "Come on, baby," and I took her into the big house and sat her down at the real table. I poured some real iced tea in the glasses and sat there with her. Then she said to me, "*Now this is a real tea party.*"

We've been playing tea party in our plastic houses too, only we call it "having church." We are forcing God to be confined within the constraints of our playhouse structures while feeding Him make-believe worship and praise. Then we look at Him and say, "Aren't we having fun?"

Daddy, We're Tired of Playing Man-Made Games

His answer is, "Yes," but it is only because He will do anything to commune with us. He will even put "His strength into captivity"[7] to come sit with us because He is so desperate for us to be with Him. But He is really waiting for us to say, "Daddy, we're tired of playing the man-made games of church. Will You take us to the big house for real communion?"

I'm tired of coming home from church with nothing changed. I'd rather come back from an encounter with God limping instead of leaping—just so my destiny is different.

You may not like the feeling of frustration, but you need to understand that *some frustrations are holy frustrations*. Just like *some hunger is holy hunger*, it is planted by God to produce something. I didn't say it; He said it: "Blessed are those who hunger and thirst."[8]

Holy hunger and blessed frustrations can produce a destiny-altering wrestling match. You should try to lose this fight...but not until you are scared by God's touch. God's touch permanently shriveled Jacob's tendon—so much so that Jews wouldn't eat "Jacob's" tendon from any animal. Hebrew dietary codes forbid eating things that have died. God put a handle of "death" in Jacob's life in order to secure his future. *Flesh-death often produces future destiny*. Your program may die for His purpose to live.

I think that we are so full with careers and agendas and man-made machinery that we have lost the simplicity of the manifested presence of God. We desperately need to take up John the Baptist's motto and put it to work in our lives: "*He must increase, but I must decrease.*"[9] It is time to call out the Jacobs who have grown so sick of themselves that they will wrestle with their destiny until they've been touched by God—*even if they come home with a permanent limp and an eternal change of heart.*

Change my heart, O God!
Change my path, I pray!

Touch me with Your rod...
So I will go *Your way.*

Endnotes

1. Genesis 32:24-26 NKJV.

2. Genesis 32:27-30 NKJV.

3. Most scholars believe that Jacob's wrestling opponent was a theophany of Jesus Christ, based on the nature of the blessing given and upon Jacob's statement, "I have seen God face to face, and my life is preserved" (Gen. 32:30b). This incident clearly shows that the Lord *permitted* Jacob to "hold his own" in the physical wrestling match to help drive home his new name and identity in the purposes of God. It was Jacob's *will* that "prevailed" through the test in his determination to pursue God until he received His blessing.

4. Duncan Campbell shared this with Alan Vincent in a personal conversation.

5. Ibid.

6. See 2 Samuel 14:28.

7. Psalm 78:61.

8. Matthew 5:6a NKJV.

9. John 3:30.

Chapter 7

Spiritual Pornography or Spiritual Intimacy?
Voyeurism or Visitation?

God spoke to a well-known minister one time and said, "I've seen your ministry, now do you want to see Mine?" *He is saying the same thing to the Church right now.* Most preachers learn how to attract a crowd early in their ministry, but *they usually don't learn it from God. We are schooled in attracting man's attention, but ignorant in how to attract God's attention.*

I know how to plan a meeting, promote an event, and preach a message for maximum "man results," but I am reluctant to follow that path anymore. I've been down that road, and I didn't really like where I saw it was going. But I must say that the real reason for my disillusionment is that I've been *ruined by His presence.* Isaiah said it, so I can say it! "I am undone."[1] The Hebrew word there means "ruined." One encounter with Him ruins your appetite for encounters with man. Worship leaders also learn how to elevate the soul with the anointing upon their gifts, and there isn't anything wrong with that. But I sometimes wonder what happened to the true worship *leaders* whose sole purpose is to lead God's people into His presence for *His* sake?

The anointing can easily draw a big crowd, but the problem with those types of man meetings is that you can curry the favor of men without ever seeking the favor of God. There is a better way, and Jesus demonstrated it with His life. The Bible says that Jesus grew in favor with *both* God and man.[2] And He always, always, *always* put God first.

Throughout His ministry, Jesus' single focus was to hear what the Father was saying and say it and to see what the Father was doing and do it.[3] That is why Jesus, and the ministers who have followed in His footsteps, never worried about drawing big crowds. If you know God and please Him through total obedience, hunger for Him will bring the crowds to you. What would happen to our meetings if we did that? *I can guarantee you that they certainly would be different from what they are now.*

I am afraid that most of our carefully orchestrated church services and revival meetings would go along just fine without God's help, approval, or appearance. Judging by the fruit of some of our endless meetings, they have already been functioning that way for a long time. What a sad commentary. It's a statement on our low hunger level that we would be satisfied with less of God than He wants us to experience.

The Temptation Is to Promise Him When You Can't Deliver Him

We have practiced and perfected the art of entertaining man, but along the way we have lost the art of entertaining God. We've already talked about the weeping zone, that place of priestly intercession between the court of man and the altar of God where we reach toward God with one hand and reach toward man with the other. Sometimes we get so involved in attracting man to our outstretched hand that we lose the desire and the ability to attract God with the other. When you can pull men toward you but you can't get God to come close anymore, the temptation is to keep promising Him though you can't deliver Him.

Spiritual Pornography or Spiritual Intimacy?

Time and again we gather large crowds of people under a plastic banner that proclaims, "Revival!" Then we become like some perpetual late night TV co-host of the church scene, saying, "Here's God!" With practiced voice inflection and hand flourishes we invite and announce Him—only we have no place for Him to sit. In our drive to please men we forgot to please God. *There's no mercy seat!*

So He never really quite shows up. He just peeps out from behind the curtains (or the lattice, as Solomon said), releasing just enough of His anointing to let you know He's there, but not enough to have a Damascus Road encounter that utterly changes you.

Part of the problem is our habit of misusing terminology to artificially raise the expectations of people. *We perpetually over-promise and under-produce.* As I said before, if someone says, "*The glory of God is here*" from an upright position, you have my permission to question the validity of the comment. We are guilty of hyping trickles into torrents—but only in our vain imaginations. When people from the world walk in, they say, "It's nice in here. It feels peaceful. Good, it is God. There's no doubt about it, it's God...*but how much of God?*" And then they walk out.

God's Hand Can Supply, But Only His Face Can Satisfy

We promise God's glory, but often at best we give a limited measure of God's anointing. God's anointing was never meant to satisfy the hunger of our souls. The anointing and the gifts empowered by it are simply tools to assist, enable, encourage, and point us back to their Source. Only God Himself can satisfy the hunger He placed within us. *His hand can supply our needs, but only His face can satisfy our deepest longings.* As we look upon His face, we are brought into union with our destiny, and we enjoy the favor of His loving gaze and the incomparable kiss of His lips.

There is a big difference between encountering the anointing of God and encountering His glory. I'm not really interested in the anointing anymore—not when it is compared to the glory of His manifest presence. I say that because it is the only way I know to help people understand the dramatic difference between the anointing and the glory of God.

The anointing of God in all its various forms has a valid purpose in His plans and purposes. The problem is that we have become so addicted to the way the anointing makes us feel that we've turned our eyes and hearts away from the glory of God's face to get more of the anointing in His hands. The anointing empowers our flesh, and it makes us feel good. *That is why the Church is filled with "anointing junkies" on **both** sides of the pulpit.* Most (but not all) the antics in our services that draw fire from the world and various segments of the Church can be traced to this odd addiction.

If you don't believe me, ask yourself why people will trample one another to get a "hot spot" in the prayer line at major conferences. Explain to me why born-again Christians will lie, scheme, and break every rule in the book to get the "best seats" in the convention hall when "Hot Evangelist What's His Name" comes to town? Honestly, there are a lot of nationally known preachers who have fan clubs nowadays. They don't call them fan clubs, of course, because that would be embarrassing, but it is true nonetheless. *This is typical behavior when preachers and their fans become addicted to the power of the anointing.*

Uncontrolled Cravings for Cheap Spiritual Thrills Become "Spiritual Pornography"

We would often rather be vicariously thrilled by God's touch on someone else's life than pursue it on our own. Or, if we are in ministry, we can become addicted to people's infatuation with us because of the anointing. It feels so good to stand in the flow.

Addiction turns even the strongest anointing into a cheap thrill. At its worst, a preacher's uncontrollable craving to minister under the anointing—and a believer's driving compulsion to receive ministry under the anointing—becomes a form of "spiritual pornography." As in the physical variety of this compulsion, "spiritual pornographers" want to get their thrills by observing the intimacy experienced by *others* rather than shouldering the responsibility of *relationship* with God. This is the only proper channel through which we are to derive personal intimacy with God. The Lord doesn't want us to be infatuated with His hands and the blessings they bring to spirit, soul, and body. He wants us to fall head over heels in love with *Him*!

We are essentially saying, "I'm not going to go into God's intimate presence for myself. I'm going to get a cheap thrill out of sharing somebody else's encounter with God. If they are graphic and dynamic, I'll get enough goose bumps to get my anointing fix." When ministers blatantly display the anointing on their life with no regard for pursuing intimacy with God Himself or for leading God's people into personal intimacy with Him, they become "spiritual exhibitionists." They are more concerned with the pleasure derived from their personal display of anointing than with pursuing God's face and ministering to Him. Those who "watch" without pursuing God themselves become mere spiritual "voyeurs" whose lives lack the genuine relationship God desires for them.

We get addicted to the anointing in the same way the children of Israel did.[4] The ministry of Moses and the miracles he did after talking with God clearly represented divine anointing, but God wanted to give the Israelites more. In Exodus 19 He invited everyone in the group to come up and hear Him speak for themselves. This was an opportunity to go *beyond the anointing* and taste of His glory for themselves. The children of Israel said, "Moses, *you* go talk to God and find out what He says. You can have the intimacy—just take some juicy pictures and bring the anointing back to us."[5] They didn't want to have a God-encounter themselves because it required a relationship that involved responsibility and a death to self.

When you pay the price to encounter God's glory up close and personal, you can't back away from what He tells you because at that point you are "married" to Him. When you get everything secondhand you can say, "It may be or it may not be God. I can't tell because it's just a 'picture of the month.' "

I have tried to send a message to my children by telling one of them to tell the others, *"Dad said." It doesn't work.* If I say, "You go tell your sister that *I said* she needs to clean up her room and rake the yard," the "messenger" of the moment loves to deliver those kinds of messages because they feel empowered, but those messages never have the same impact as the real thing. I can still remember hearing my daughters tell one another after a "second person message" was delivered, *"You're not the boss of me!"* We say that (or the adult equivalent) to our pastors, spiritual leaders, and bosses constantly even though we are adults. All that stops when the heavenly Father shows up personally and manifests His glory.

The Addicted Are Consumed With Their Next Anointing "Fix"

If they don't watch it, preachers can become a major obstacle to "God coming down" in their churches because they are addicted to the anointing. They would rather preach than worship Him until His glory comes in. The truth is that our best sermons can never equal just one word spoken directly to us from God Himself. Congregations can become just as addicted to the anointing that flows from their gifted leaders or from the gifts resident in the congregation. The addicted are all too consumed with getting their next anointing fix to worry about seeking the face of God.

"Why doesn't God just take back the anointed gifts He gives those addicted preachers?" He doesn't work that way. Once He opens that door of anointing in a person's life, His gifts and callings are without repentance.[6] Once a preacher goes over the line into pure anointing addiction, God won't "hold them back" by removing His gift. He simply backs away from them personally because *He is more committed to character than to talent.*

When the character runs out and the talent or gifting continues, a person is skating on thin ice, and eventually he or she will fall through. Any gift from God that is separated from His abiding presence will deteriorate over time. (That may be a pretty good description of what has happened to many of the great denominations in the Church that were founded upon solid truths and genuine experiences in God at one time.) Why don't these spiritually bankrupt ministers just go back to their first love? They want to keep standing up before the people even when they know that their private testimony doesn't match their public anointing.

We Have Prostituted the Very Processes of God

Let me assure you that there is a big difference between a one-dimensional representation and the real thing. We have prostituted the very processes of God by pursuing what comes from a man as the complete representation of God. Some people talk about things of the spirit as if they were there, but they are only talking about what they've heard. They have not had a legitimate encounter themselves, so their description of God comes across in a flat, single dimension. That's the difference between looking at a picture of your child or stroking the hair of that toddler you love.

The Church has perverted and prostituted its anointing by chasing after the approval of man when that's not the real purpose for the anointing. When God first introduced Moses to the anointing oil, He said,

*And you shall make from these a holy anointing oil, an ointment compounded according to the art of the perfumer. It shall be a holy anointing oil. With it you shall anoint the tabernacle of meeting and the ark of the Testimony; the table and all its utensils, the lampstand and its utensils, and the altar of incense; the altar of burnt offering with all its utensils, and the laver and its base. You shall consecrate them, that they may be most holy; whatever touches them must be holy. **And you shall anoint Aaron and his sons,** and consecrate them, that they may minister to Me as priests. And you shall speak to the children of Israel, saying: "This shall be a holy anointing oil to Me*

Consecrate =

*throughout your generations. **It shall not be poured on man's flesh; nor shall you make any other like it**, according to its composition. It is holy, and it shall be holy to you."*[7]

It seems incongruous that the Scripture says, "shall anoint" and "not...on man's flesh" in the same passage. Not on unconsecrated flesh! Dedicated death-to-self flesh is ready to be anointed.

Psalm 133 shows us *how* this anointing oil was used when it says, "It is like the precious ointment upon the head, that ran down upon the beard, even Aaron's beard: that went down to the skirts of his garments."[8] The Israelites made the anointing oil by the quart because when it was time to anoint something, they poured, smeared, drenched, and on occasion sprinkled heavily. Just think about Aaron, the high priest.

Quart Poured

Are You Ready for God to Ruin Your Carpet?

How much oil would you have to pour over a grown man's head (perhaps a man who was careful *not* to cut his hair) to make it run down his beard (a full beard), and then run down his full-length priestly linen garments so generously that it drips off the hem to the ground at his feet? I don't know how much it would take, but I can guarantee you that if God recreated that event in your church, *it would ruin your carpet*. (And whoever stood in proxy for Aaron would need a new hairdo.)

I want the kind of messy services that have "*divine intervention*" stamped all over them. When men anoint men for man's approval, they use just enough to win the applause and raise the goose bumps. When God anoints man, He nearly drowns us with His fragrance just so *He can stand to come near.*

YOU CAN'T SEEK HIS FACE AND SAVE YOURS. YOU MAY LOSE YOUR DIGNITY IN YOUR PURSUIT OF HIS DEITY.

Spiritual Pornography or Spiritual Intimacy?

[handwritten: acts 2:]

That is the way the "first church service" went. Read the second chapter of Acts and explain to me why the disciples stumbled and staggered out of an upper room so inebriated in the Spirit that people accused them of being falling-down drunks. *How seeker-friendly was that?* Peter had to refute the accusations with the logic of a lawyer and power from on high to tell them, "Look, it's too early. The bars aren't even opened. And smell our breath, anyway." Seeker-friendly or not, the first church of 120 Spirit-filled drunks held an altar call, and 3,000 people came to Christ. *[handwritten: 3,000 people got saved]*

We need to see that happen in some of our services. I'd love to see God's anointing wreck us and wreck the church. I'd love to see people stagger out of the building just dripping with oil. I can tell you this much: We wouldn't look sane, we wouldn't look normal, and we certainly wouldn't be considered "seeker-friendly." But a service like that can only happen because God showed up. Which would you chose—*clean carpet or clean heart, nice hair or an oily but fragrant mess*?

We Maintain Our Composure at the Cost of Our Convictions

Does it shock you when I tell you that the world is tired of the "normal church"? It may be all that we have, but it hasn't done the job. I am not saying that we need to become a bunch of mindless fanatics, but the truth is that *our greatest temptation is the desire to maintain our composure at the cost of our convictions.*

We are not where we ought to be, and we are not doing what we ought to do. Why? *Because we think we have a reputation to maintain.* Reputations mean nothing to God. I am thinking of a King who made Himself of *no reputation* and took on the form of a servant just so He could do what He needed to do.[9] *You can't seek His face and save yours. You may lose your dignity in your pursuit of His deity.*

Frankly, I've noticed that we need those unpredictable services that force us to lose our composure because that is often the only way we will allow God to break something open. *Again, you may lose your dignity in your pursuit of His deity.* When the people of God commit themselves to see the heavens open in their church and city, they become *pregnant with the purposes of God.* Those people will inevitably end up in a "birthing room" when the divine matrix of Heaven will open to release the glory of God.

If you have never been there, let me assure you that the typical birthing room is not a place of composure. I have been there in the natural as chief spectator (my wife was the participator). I learned firsthand that a woman goes to death's door to bring back life. In the same way, Calvary was not a place of composure. *It was a bloody birthing ground in which the Son of God went to the grave and back to bring us new life.*

We've Sanitized the Cross and Reduced the Cost of Commitment

The "church with a reputation" has managed to come up with "salvation in a package" where converts simply walk up front and shake somebody's hand in one neat and tidy event. Sometimes churches will even provide hankies to dab the tear that may or may not form in the corner of one's eye. I understand the thinking behind all that, but I have a nagging image of how our salvation was originally delivered. I keep seeing the beaten Christ robed in bloody garments, and I wonder if we've sanitized the cross and reduced the cost of commitment too much. He died naked, indicating a total loss of dignity. Even in the throes of dying! *He lost His dignity, and we seek to preserve ours.* God is actively courting our love, but we think that things get too messy the way they are. We want to sanitize revival until it can be offered to people in a simple, shrink-wrapped, mass-produced package that is nice and tidy. Unfortunately for man's pride, *some of the things that make God comfortable also tend to make men incredibly uncomfortable.*

When is somebody going to shoulder the burden and say, "Pour the oil on me until my hair is messed up and it drips off of everything I touch. Drench me in Your presence until everything I'm around becomes an oily mess and I don't even look or act the same. *Disable me with Your touch until I walk with a limp.* It will change the way my brother looks at me. Pour it on me"? Let me stumble from the upper room into the lower streets. The "birthing room," called the upper room, disgorged uncomposed disciples to forever change the world.

Forget Shortcuts: Keep the Main Thing the Main Thing

Don't bother to look for shortcuts to revival or a revelation of God's glory. If you want to pursue God, then you will have to do it the same way they wooed and won, and chased and pursued Him in the past. *There is no new method or path to revival.* We just need to rediscover God's original recipe and quit dabbling. *We have majored on the minors* for so long that we have lost the pursuit of God Himself. Let me share with you some wise counsel my father gave me: *The main thing is to keep the main thing the main thing.* The main thing is Him, the centrality of Christ!

The Song of Solomon reveals the real purpose of the anointing. The Bridegroom calls to His Bride and says, "How much better than wine is your love, and the scent of your perfumes than all spices!"[10] The true anointing should cause God to say to His Bride, the Church, "The way you smell to Me ravished My heart." There is something about the fragrant anointing on the prayers, praise, and worship of the saints that intrigues God.

If we can direct the sweet fragrance of our anointing and our sacrifice of praise upwards toward Heaven instead of horizontally toward one another, we may see the heavens open. There are at least 131 references to "anointing, anointed, or anoint" in the Old Testament and 18 in the New Testament. The anointing has several different purposes in the New Testament:

1. Most New Testament references mark the anointing of Jesus for His ministry, death, and burial as the Lamb of God, the Divine Sacrifice.[11]
2. Sometimes it signifies the empowerment of human beings for divine works among men (or of kings to rule under God's authority).[12]

3. At times it signifies God's seal upon men.[13]
4. It releases God's power for healing or deliverance (representing a measure of God's virtue on loan to bring glory to Him and Him alone).[14]
5. On rare occasions, it is God's way of setting apart and blessing anointed people (like Jesus) for total devotion to righteousness and the things of God.[15]
6. In John's Epistle, it is a gift we receive from Jesus that abides in us and teaches us all things.[16]

We Prostitute the Anointing Because We Want to Smell Good

The primary purpose of the anointing in both the Old and New Testaments was to separate things and people and make them acceptable to God (and occasionally for kings). Unfortunately, we tend to prostitute the anointing because we want to smell good for everybody else.

According to the second chapter of the Book of Esther, after the wife of King Ahasuerus of Persia refused to show herself to his drunken banquet guests, he launched a kingdom-wide search for a new queen. A Jewish maiden named Esther was selected to be one of the candidates for the king's harem. As I said in *The God Chasers*, Esther and the other prospective brides spent "one year in preparation for one night with the king."[17]

Esther spent six months soaking in oil of myrrh and six more months soaking in other added sweet odors to purify and prepare her for one night with the king. All but one of the candidates would see the king once and rarely if ever see him again. The Bible says, "And the king loved Esther above all the women, and she obtained *grace* and *favour* in his sight more than all the virgins; so that he set the royal crown upon her head, and made her queen...."[18]

Esther also "obtained *favour* in the sight of all them that looked upon her."[19] Can you imagine what Esther smelled like after spending a year soaking in the anointing oil? It was on her garments and embedded in her skin and hair. Everywhere she walked she left a cloud of incense, and the smell of precious myrrh was on her. When she walked through the palace, every man in the place raised his eyebrows at her and said, "Oh, look! Look at Esther."

Esther Was After the Approval of the King Himself

I don't think Esther returned a single glance or flirtatious wink. She didn't want to waste all the time she had spent in the anointing just to win the approval of men; *she was after the approval of the king himself.* Can we say the same for the Church, the Bride of Christ? We have grown accustomed to wearing God's anointing to win the approval of the King's court instead of the King Himself. In Moses' day, the anointing was reserved for the things of God and sanctified or set apart flesh. To anoint anything else was sin. Too many people would squander the anointing on unsanctified, unrepentant flesh to win man's approval. *The anointing can only make putrified flesh smell better temporarily if the root is a rotten and unrepentant, proud heart.*

If you are a preacher, a teacher, a worship leader, or hold any position of responsibility in the local body, don't waste God's precious anointing by running after man's approval. Use it to prepare the Bride for the King.

The purpose of the anointing is to bring God and man together in holy communion. Moses knew the difference between the anointing and the glory. He had the anointing of God. He knew the thrill of working miracles and signs and wonders through the anointing. Moses had a good thing, but he asked God for the best thing. He said, "Please, show me Your glory."[20]

I must admit, I feel the same way Moses did (although I won't compare my ministry to his). The evidence of God's power in the anointing isn't enough anymore. The gifts, blessings, and provisions of His hands are appreciated, but I want more. *I want Him. I long to see His glory and dwell in His manifest presence more than I long for the blessings of His hands.*

Like Moses, we have an opportunity to go beyond God's omnipresence and anointing to see God's glory. Our spirits were instantly transformed into new creations at salvation, but we still need to do something about our sin-tainted bodies and messy souls before God can expose us to His shining glory. The blood of Jesus covers our sin and preserves us from death, but that doesn't mean we are particularly attractive to God apart from the fragrant covering cloud of repentant, broken worship.

God's Glory Lingers Behind the Blood-Soaked Doorway of Repentance

Moses wasn't allowed to see God's glory until after his flesh had died. As I mentioned repeatedly in *The God Chasers*, my first book, *the New Testament equivalent of death is repentance.* We may not like it, but the glory of God lingers behind the blood-soaked doorway of repentance. If we ever want to enter into the manifested glory of the presence of God, we will have to walk through the door called repentance.

We like to avoid repentance by claiming it was all taken care of the day we received Jesus. Yes, the Lord did His part on the cross, but you and I aren't finished yet. Repentance is an on-going, daily requirement in the life of every disciple of Christ. That is why Jesus said, "If any man will come after Me, let him deny himself, and take up his cross **daily** [let him *die* to self through daily repentance], and follow Me."[21]

We like to take pompous stands behind our pulpits, point at the sin-choked world, and command them to repent. Will we ever learn that we will never be able to force the world into repentance—especially when the same problems exist inside the Church that exist in the world. We are standing on fake platforms of hypocrisy that will soon crumble. *The Church must no longer point toward repentance; we must lead the way with a lifestyle of repentance.* We must embrace repentance as a body.

God uses His anointing to train us, cleanse us, heal us, and prepare us for His manifest presence in ways reminiscent of the way the king's chamberlain prepared Esther for the king of

Persia. In the end, the anointing takes us back to the altar of God and the place of repentance. Repentance, in turn, can usher in the very glory of God.

The Anointing Is About Us; the Glory Is About Him

If you are anointed, you will preach better, pray better, minister better, and worship better and with greater freedom, but that is not His highest purpose. *The anointing is all about us, but the glory is all about Him.* The anointing refers to what He pours, smears, or places upon us to help us do His will. Sometimes it acts as a "perfume" to prepare us for intimacy, as in Esther's case.[22] When the anointing of God rests on you, it makes whatever you do "better." It doesn't matter whether you preach, sing, witness, usher, pray, or minister to the babies in the back. When the anointing comes upon you, it empowers your gifts, talents, and callings with the power of God. Nevertheless, it is still the anointing, and it rests on flesh.

The glory is different. When the glory of God comes, you suddenly and clearly understand why God said "no flesh should glory in His presence."[23] A more literal translation of this passage might be, "no flesh should glory in God's face."[24] I can testify from personal experience and prove from the Scriptures that when the glory comes, your flesh can't do anything. Have you noticed that when people have a "God encounter" in the Bible, they usually end up on their face? *It is because they didn't really have a choice.*

The difference between the anointing of God and the glory of God is like the difference between the tiny blue spark of static electricity and the raw power of a 440-volt power line overhead or a lightning strike on your head! We are so busy rubbing our feet across the carpet of God's promises and giving one another tiny blue sparks of anointing that we don't realize God wants to jolt us with His 440-volt glory line from Heaven. The one will thrill you a little, but you get the feeling the other might kill you or change your life forever.

The Anointing in and of Itself
Won't Get the Job Done

I love the anointing of God, and I am thankful for every good gift He has given us. Yet I am convinced God's first choice is for us to seek His face of favor rather than His hand of anointing. I've spent most of my life in church (multiple services up to five days per week since childhood). Personally, I've had enough anointed preaching and singing to last me two lifetimes. It's good and it's thrilling, but I must tell you the anointing in and of itself is not going to get the job done. *We must have the manifest presence of God Himself on display for the world.*

God Wants a Church That Has Eyes Only for Him

Failure to discern between the good and the best can cause us to make uneven trades. *Esther refused to trade the winking approval of men in the king's court for the favor of the king himself.* As a result, the king told Esther right in front of her enemy, "What is your petition? It shall be granted you. What is your request, up to half the kingdom? It shall be done!"[25] *God is looking for a Bride-Church that has eyes only for Him.* Then He will delight in giving her the key to the city and the life of the nation.

Don't make the mistake of prostituting the anointing to pursue man so your church will grow. Just say, "I care more for His presence than His presents. I elevate 'glory' above growth." No, that is not heresy. My Bible doesn't contain a single instance of God acting worried about the size of His Church. If things go right, you don't have to worry about the church growing. Just get serious about pursuing Him. Perfume yourself with the anointing and enter into such heated worship toward Him that you don't care who is there and who is not.[26]

Set your sights on the goal of breaking open the heavens to behold His glory over your city and nation. It is easy to mark the churches that have learned how to focus anointing vertically for God's favor instead of horizontally toward men.

Just look for the glory-filled footprints of God leading to their door.

They have had a visitation.

Endnotes

1. Isaiah 6:5.
2. Luke 2:52.
3. See John 5:30; 7:16-18; 8:28-29; 12:49-50.
4. See Exodus 19.
5. Exodus 20:19, paraphrase.
6. See Romans 11:29.
7. Exodus 30:25-32 NKJV.
8. Psalm 133:2.
9. See Philippians 2:7.
10. Song of Solomon 4:10b NKJV.
11. See Mark 14:8; 16:1; Luke 7:46.
12. See Luke 4:18; Acts 10:38.
13. See 2 Corinthians 1:21.
14. See Mark 6:13; John 9:6; James 5:14-15.
15. See Hebrews 1:9.
16. See 1 John 2:27.
17. Tommy Tenney, *The God Chasers* (Shippensburg, PA: Destiny Image Publishers, 1998), 41.
18. Esther 2:17.
19. Esther 2:15.
20. Exodus 33:18 NKJV.
21. Luke 9:23.
22. This understanding is clearly supported in the Old Testament uses of the Hebrew word for anointing, *shemen,* and in the New Testament Greek word, *aleipho.* The word *glory* (the Hebrew word *kabowd* or *kabod*) always refers to the weighty presence of God Himself. The only way to see or experience the glory is for God Himself to show up in the house. Hebrew and Greek word definitions were drawn from the work of James Strong, *Strong's Exhaustive Concordance of the Bible* (Peabody, MA: Hendrickson Publishers, n.d.), **anointing** (#H8081, H8080; and #G218, G3045), and **glory** (#H3519, H3513; and #G1391).
23. 1 Corinthians 1:29.

24.   This expanded meaning is drawn from the literal meaning of the Greek word *enopion,* translated as "presence" in First Corinthians 1:29. It means "in the face of" God. Strong, *Strong's Exhaustive Concordance,* **presence** (#G1799).

25.   Esther 5:6b NKJV.

26.   Please understand that this comment refers specifically to those moments when you are focused upon ministering to God. I would never advocate that you be insensitive or harsh toward others or become rebellious toward leadership in the name of "deeper worship." I'm referring to what I call "the Mary/Martha" balance. Both women were doing the right things in Luke 10:38-42, but Martha simply needed to understand that when the Master is in the house, that is the time to drop everything else and minister to Him. Otherwise, the practical duties of servanthood and preparation in the house are absolutely necessary and proper. In those times when Jesus was *not* in the house, it would have been improper for Mary to sit while Martha worked.

Chapter 8

The Day the Music Died
(And the Day It Will Be Resurrected)

Dear Sister "B" was a real wonder to me when I was growing up.[1] My grandfather and my father co-pastored a church in Louisiana, and at times when the spiritual climate got a little tough in a service, they would confer and then call for Sister "B" to sing.

Now that didn't make much sense to me because Sister "B's" voice sounded something like a disharmonious foghorn. I just couldn't stand her singing and neither could the other kids, so we used to make fun of her (secretly, of course). Now I'm a little bit wiser. *I've learned that if God's presence can turn a peasant into a princess, then He can definitely use the Sister "Bs" of the world.*

I can tell you that I've been in hundreds of "ark-less" meetings as a minister of the gospel when I wished I could call for Sister "B." You see, my father and grandfather knew what they were doing. They called for her because every time that sister began to sing, tears would start rolling and the hardness of the service would be shattered. For some reason, when Sister "B" stood up to sing to God, the presence of God would suddenly be ushered in.

It was obvious that even though we didn't like Sister "B's" singing, God liked the notes she was hitting. That was because Sister "B's" high notes had very little to do with the raucous tones assaulting our fleshly ears. Worshipers take note: *It wasn't the almost melodious quality of Sister "B's" voice that made a difference; it was the flawless melody pouring from her heart that made the difference.*

It seemed like every time Sister "B" stood up and sang, the presence of God would enter. There was no obvious connection between her physical voice and the sudden approach of God's presence that could be perceived with earthly eyes and ears. The beautiful melody that attracted God to our little church "on the wrong side of the society tracks" could only be heard with the "ear" of the inner man, the spiritual hearing organ of the heart. This is what Jesus was talking about when He said, "He that hath an ear, let him hear what the Spirit saith."[2] He was not talking about the fleshly appendages on the side of our heads. He was referring to the spiritual hearing organ to which God whispers and speaks.

God Didn't Want to Miss a Single Note of Sister "B's" Lullaby

The key to Sister "B's" anointing was the fact that she was a worshiper. When she stood up to sing, she was oblivious to the row of snickering boys and the other people in the pews. She sang directly to God as an act of pure worship for His own pleasure, period. As a result, God didn't want to miss a single note of her lullaby to Him (in spite of our boyish prayers that she would stop). He just had to move His seat a little closer every time Sister "B" began to worship Him.

If we're not careful, we can get so enmeshed in the machinery of "having church" and having a good time that we forget the purpose of worship. Our general opinion of worship is often expressed with the statement, "Well, I'm going to be a little late for church. I'll miss the worship, but I'll get there for the Word."

AS FAR AS GOD IS CONCERNED, WORSHIP IS HIS PART, AND THE WORD IS OUR PART.

What we fail to realize is that as far as God is concerned, *worship is His part,* and *the Word is our part.* That means that if we miss the worship, we've missed His best part where we give to Him. Instead we selfishly skip God's part and only show up to have our itching ears tickled.

"Well, God appreciates the Word." Oh yes, I know, but I want to ask you a serious question: *Do you really think God gets anything out of our preaching?* Do you think He might learn something about Himself from our anointed teaching? (The answer might be yes, but for the wrong reason. He probably listens to our preaching and says, *"Did I say that? I don't remember saying it quite that way...."*)

God doesn't get anything out of our preaching. *I am not saying that the preaching of God's Word isn't important.* I am saying that worship is more important to God than preaching because worship builds the basket or container for the fresh bread of Heaven. If you build a mercy seat, then you can have the glory of God come in, and worship is what builds the seat of God. Ask yourself this question: "What is the priority of Heaven?" To talk *to* Him or talk *about* Him?

Is Our Favorite Hymn: "Give Me, Give Me, Give Me"?

In our miscalculated valuation of what "church" is all about, we think in terms of what we receive from it instead of what we give to Him. As a result, we have turned "church" into a selfish proposition. I am going to make a bold statement that will anger some folks: *We have turned church into glorified bless me clubs where we come with our hands extended and a long laundry list of wants. We might as well start with our favorite hymn: "Give me, give me, give me."*

That sets up a serious clash and conflict because God comes to church with His heart hungry. Tell me, what does God eat when He gets hungry? The answer may surprise you. Jesus gives us the answer during His encounter with the Samaritan woman at the well in chapter 4 of John's Gospel.

Jesus had an appointment with a Samaritan woman at Jacob's well in the Samaritan city of Sychar, which means "intoxicating drink."[3] The disciples weren't in a waiting mood because they were preoccupied with their grumbling fleshly stomachs. Can you picture Jesus leaning against a raised wall at Jacob's well, looking at the wristwatch of eternity and saying to Himself, "She should be coming any moment now." God the Son had an appointment with a woman of the world. *She had a blind date with destiny and didn't even know about it.*

Perhaps you can remember the day and time your destiny intercepted with deity—did you have any idea that you were about to have a God encounter? *That is because God set the appointment and you didn't.* While Jesus waited for the Samaritan woman to show up, His disciples were rubbing their bellies. (They weren't good "waiters" then, and we don't do any better today.) They said something like, "Jesus, we saw a Burger King right down the road there. We're going to get something to eat. We'll bring You something back, is that okay?" Jesus just told them, "Go on, I'm going to wait right here."

The Woman of Rejection Had an Appointment With Perfection

Jesus probably watched the disciples pass the Samaritan woman in the road on their way to get food. (The disciples seemed to have a knack of missing momentous moments.) The woman who approached Jacob's well had been living a life of rejection. The Bible clearly tells us that she came at the noon hour (the sixth hour), and the women typically came in the morning to draw water for cooking and in the evening to draw water for bathing and washing. I think she wanted to avoid the biting remarks and judgmental stares of the women of the town.

Jesus saw past this woman's multiple husbands and saw the need of her heart. She admitted to having several husbands but made no mention of children. Perhaps this indicates that she was a barren woman who had no children. Is it possible that she went from husband to husband searching for someone to give her children? *Did she go through all that pain only to recognize in the end that the problem rested with her?*

As this woman walked up to Jacob's well, she probably thought she had run into something far worse than the sharp tongues of the townswomen—there was a Jewish rabbi waiting there. I can almost hear her thoughts: *He's probably a Pharisee who keeps every jot and tittle of the ancient law of Moses—including the requirement not to have any dealings with Samaritans.* Then the inconceivable happened: The Jewish holy man said, "I would like some water."

She expected to be rejected, but she wasn't prepared for Jesus' request. She said, "How can You ask me that? You are a Jew, and Jews aren't supposed to even speak to us."[4] In that moment, Jesus embarked on an intricate journey of leading a soul to a place of hunger by asking questions and making intriguing statements that drew her deeper into the conversation.

> *"If you knew the gift of God, and who it is who says to you, 'Give Me a drink,' you would have asked Him, and He would have given you living water." The woman said to Him, "Sir, You have nothing to draw with, and the well is deep. Where then do You get that living water?"*[5]

Jesus Was Talking About Living Water and Worship

Jesus ultimately helped the woman understand that He wasn't talking about the kind of water found in Jacob's well. He was talking about living water and worship. He revealed the purpose for their divine appointment when He said,

> *"Woman, believe Me, the hour is coming when you will neither on this mountain, nor in Jerusalem, worship the Father....But the hour is coming, and now is, when the **true worshipers** will*

> *the Father in spirit and truth; for **the Father is seek-** **h** to worship Him. God is Spirit, and those who worship* *Him must worship in spirit and truth."*[6]

That Samaritan woman had walked to Jacob's well with a thirst for well water, but she wound up meeting the Well of Life and discovered she was really thirsty for living water. Jesus told her, "The Father is seeking such to worship Him." The *only thing that the Father is actively seeking is worshipers!*

There Will Be No Pastors in Heaven

This encounter with the woman at the well is a picture of God's unceasing search for worshipers. Do you realize there will be no pastors in Heaven? There will be no apostles, preachers, evangelists, Sunday school superintendents, church board members, elders, or deacons in Heaven either. That is because the only "job description" in Heaven is that of a worshiper. On earth you can be a both a pastor and a worshiper, or a Sunday school teacher and a worshiper, but you must understand that your primary calling is to worship the Father in spirit and in truth. *What you do in the vineyard may vary, but all real sons and daughters passionately love their father.*

God knows all things—and He knows where everything is hidden. He doesn't need gold or precious gems, but He knows where every single ounce of gold is hidden and can place His finger on every gemstone embedded in the bedrock of the earth. Yet there is one commodity that is more precious than all the others put together for which God searches unceasingly—a worshiper who freely offers love, praise, worship, and adoration to God in spirit and truth. The pure worship of His children made in His image is exceptionally rare because it comes from only one source in all the created universe—us! Our worship is hidden under the rock of the will of man—and God refuses to violate our will and move that rock.

God is on a mission to populate Heaven with worshipers for a very good reason. When lucifer fell from glory, I believe a crucial aspect of heavenly worship fell with him. If you were used to listening to a quartet sing in four-part harmony, you would immediately miss something if one of the voices dropped out. You know what it used to sound like and what it was supposed to sound like. The moment one of those voices is removed, you would say, "Well, that's good, but there is something missing."

God Misses the Song of the Heart

God remembers when lucifer and the sons of the morning used to sing His praises with unearthly beauty and power. It *is as if* He says, "When will that be restored?" He is still surrounded by six-winged seraphim who unceasingly declare His glory, but He misses the song of the heart.

Despite years of research, *I cannot find a single place in the Bible where music is mentioned as a part of Heaven's environment after the fall of satan.*[7] I have asked numerous theologians about this. Most people respond to my statement by saying, "Well, Tommy, you remember what the angels sang at the birth of Christ in Bethlehem, don't you? They sang, 'Glory to God in the highest, peace on earth, good will toward men.' "

At that point I have to gently direct them back to the biblical passages in the Gospels. "No, if you read it carefully, you will see that the Bible doesn't say they sang. I really hate to mess up all our wonderful Christmas plays and holiday hymns. It won't hurt a thing to let your little children dress up as little angels and sing in a Christmas cantata, so don't worry about it. I just want you to know what the Bible actually says":

> *And suddenly there was with the angel a multitude of the heavenly host* **praising** *God, and* **saying,** *Glory to God in the highest, and on earth peace, good will toward men.*[8]

Job 38:7 says, "When the morning stars *sang* together, and all the sons of God shouted for joy." The context clearly places this event at the very creation of our universe *just before lucifer's fall.*[9] After the fall, I can't find any literal Bible reference to singing or music in Heaven. I don't have a problem with people who say, "Well, I had a vision and heard angels singing"; I am just saying that I can't find it mentioned in the Bible once satan was ejected from Heaven.

If music fell when satan fell, then that explains why the bulk of the satanic influence in our world comes from the realm of music. Music is his venue, so we shouldn't be surprised that the first place problems often show up in most churches is in the area of music and worship. Obviously, not all music "comes from satan," but he exerts great influence through music. This also explains something else...

The Church spends countless hours crafting sermons, arranging music scores, and rehearsing choirs and singers to make sure they are just right. Yet no matter how much energy we spend pursuing excellence in those areas, I must tell you we will never compete with the world's symphony orchestras or the bands and artists featured on MTV or VH1. In fact, we are not supposed to compete in those arenas!

Before you slam this book shut and toss it in the garbage can, I want you to understand something:

Our music may never be as good as the world's music because our value system is different from the world's.

We are not after perfection so much as we are after Presence.

When the Church turns all its focus and energies toward the technical and professional perfection of our well-rehearsed music, our crafted sermons, and our tightly scripted services, we can unknowingly begin competing in the wrong arena. We need to stick with the one arena in which no one can compete with us—the art and ability to pull down the manifest presence of God. *Technical perfection may win the praise of men, but only the anointing and glory of God can melt their hardened hearts.*

At some point we've got to turn man's volume down and turn God's volume up. A Damascus Road encounter will turn a murderer like Saul into a martyr named Paul in less than 30 seconds. Perfected music won't do that, but *perfected praise* might attract Him, and His presence will!

Why Is God Attracted to Our Pitiful Praise?

For all these reasons, I believe that music fell when satan fell. Could it mean that when God wants to hear that aspect of worship, *He has to come to earth to hear it*? I don't want to offend anyone, but I have to ask this question everywhere I go: *Have you ever wondered why God is attracted to our pitiful praise?*

The Lord used my youngest daughter to answer this question for me. Wherever I go, I carry a priceless work of art along with me in my briefcase. Sometimes I will pull it out in airports just to look at it and finger it. It isn't an oil painting, nor is it done in pastels or charcoal. It is what I call the "scrawled pencil on yellow legal pad" medium. The hand-scribbled text on this piece of art is usually hard for most people to read, but I have the fatherly gift of interpretation! Frankly, the writing is really pitiful, but you can just make out the words:

> *"I Love god.*
> *To god*
> *fum*
> *Andrea Tenney."*

It's really pitiful by adult standards and it wouldn't mean anything to you, but it is priceless to me. Someday it will join a whole box full of other scribbled crayon masterpieces back home, and every one of them is special to me. What makes those things precious to me? It isn't that they are so artistically done, and it isn't the quality of the "writing" that endears these drawings to my heart; *it is who drew them!* It is my relationship to the child.

The crayon drawings from my children wouldn't mean anything to you, and the crayon drawings from your youngsters wouldn't mean anything to me. In the same way, the angels in Heaven who surround the orb of God's throne with ceaseless praise and magnificent worship scratch their heads when suddenly the Deity leans forward and says, "Shhhh!" When they fall into an obedient hushed silence, He says, "I think I hear something...."

Everything Stops When God Almighty Hears Our Pitiful Refrain

The six-winged seraphim were simply doing what they were created to do. They were crying out the praises of God in perfection and beating the atmosphere with their wings while covering their faces and their feet in humility. Then everything stops when God Almighty hears a pitiful refrain rising faintly from the chaos of the earth below: "He is holy, He is holy...." He quickly commands the angelic hosts, "Be quiet." (I can almost hear the angels in the rear whisper to one another, "*There He goes again.*")

Can you see the archangels Michael and Gabriel conversing, as they say, "I don't know what gets into Him. Every time He hears them, He does this. That is such pitiful praise...."? We think we're doing so well when we paint a masterpiece, when the quartet hits the final note in its best four-part harmony, when the choir brings the crowd to its feet. Meanwhile, the angelic hosts who once heard lucifer the archangel rattle the heavens with thunderous worship and breathtaking celestial music are saying, "*What is man that You are mindful of him, and the son of man that You visit him?*"[10]

Oblivious to every whispered question, God hushes the angels and says to Michael and Gabriel,

"Look, guys, I'm going to have to leave it with you."
"Why? What is it, Lord?"
"Well, you see, I heard something that I just can't ignore. I heard the song of the redeemed again..."

The Almighty Leaves His Throne to Join a Huddle of Prostrate Worshipers

In the twinkling of an eye, the manifest presence of God is transported from Heaven to the middle of a huddle of prostrate worshipers gathered in a tear-stained circle singing, "Holy, holy, holy is the Lord...." *God leaves His magnificent throne of Heaven and comes to earth to be enthroned on the pitiful praises of His people.* We may think our praise and worship services are wonderful while the angels in Heaven are saying, "I don't understand. That is just a pitiful crayon drawing compared to what we do in Heaven." God isn't attracted by the quality of our worship or our musical ability. *It is because of who we are.* He is attracted because of His relationship to the worshipers. We're His children!

I can almost hear Him explaining to Michael and Gabriel, "Now, I know they can't sing or make the heavenly music you heard when lucifer was here. I know they can't say it like you say it, but those are My sons and daughters." Jesus had to explain it to the Pharisees too. He told them, "Have you never read, 'Out of the mouth of babes and nursing infants You have perfected praise'?"[11]

Who can resist the sound of the lisping little voice of a two-year-old-saying, "*Daddy, I wuv you.*" It isn't the perfection of their diction that melts our hearts. We aren't moved by the sheer oratorical skill of their delivery. It is the heart of simple passion that causes us to sweep that child up into our arms in a wave of emotion.

So when we lift up our "crayon drawings" to Heaven with the clumsily scrawled words, "I luv You God, fum Tommy Tenney," He leaves the throne of Heaven and is literally enthroned upon our pitiful praise. God says, "It's not how pretty they do it. It's just that they are My offspring." *He would rather hear you stumble through a song with a voice like a cracked foghorn than to hear the six-winged seraphim surround Him with chants of "holy" in tones of heavenly perfection.*

We Will Sing a Song the Angels Cannot Sing

Music may have fallen from Heaven when the angelic worship leader was ejected for rebellion, but God had a plan for restoring Heaven's music through His redemption plan for man. Satan isn't the only being equipped and anointed to sing to the Most High. Our praise and worship may sound pitiful to angelic ears, but the Bible says that when we enter that holy city, we will sing a song the angels cannot sing.[12] When we enter singing the song of Moses and the song of the redeemed, the heavenly host is going to fall into a stunned silence for 30 minutes, as if they will be commenting, "*We've never heard it like this.*"

Lucifer was cast out of Heaven because he wanted to illegally ascend to God's level and sit on His throne. God has decreed that the redeemed saints of the Lamb will be seated on the throne with Him—right where lucifer wanted to be and couldn't. God is literally going to use imperfect praisers to embarrass lucifer, the fallen morning star. *Man, who was made a little lower than the angels, is going to be elevated higher than all the angelic host* and will sit on the throne of God together with Him.[13]

Jesus Said, "I Think I Found One..."

Do you know what God eats when He's hungry? *Worship.* Do you remember the woman at the well? When Jesus told her about His living water and said that His Father was seeking true worshipers, she gave the answer He was looking for. She said,

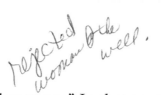
rejected by the woman at the well.

"I want that water." In that moment Jesus might have mused, *I think I found one. That is what I was waiting for.*

When the disciples came back, they said, "Lord, we've got Your Burger King for You," or "Here's Your McDonalds Big Mac, Master." They were shocked when He said, "I'm not hungry. I've had meat to eat you don't know of." It was as if He were thinking, *You wouldn't understand it, but I've been receiving worship from a rejected woman at the well. I've done My Father's will and found a worshiper. After that feast, I don't need anything you have for Me.*[14]

God comes to earth because His growling hunger pains for worship draw Him to the imperfect praise of His children, who say, "*I luv You, Daddy.*" He isn't particularly impressed with our polished singing and multimillion dollar buildings. It is all pitiful by celestial standards, but it is precious to Him because He loves us.

"Red and yellow, black and white,
They are precious in His sight.
Jesus loves the *little children* of the world."

He comes because we hold up childlike imperfect praise with hearts full of love—like a child reaching up and a Father reaching down.

He is out to populate Heaven with worshipers who can fulfill that missing part that has been absent ever since lucifer fell. Jesus auditioned the woman at the well in search of that "high note" of transparency and purity. He gave her the opportunity to answer a question for which He already knew the answer: *Can you hit this note?* He wondered, as He searched under the "rock of the human will" for a worshiper. Then He told the woman, *Highest Note is worship from a True heart*
"Go get your husband." *To the LORD Jesus Christ.*

She could have hidden her sin or covered her broken life with the fig leaves of a lie, but for once in her life she thought, *No, I know it's not very pretty, but I'm going to tell Him the truth.* Then she said, "I have no husband." *God in LORD Jesus Christ is the only one to sit on the Throne, you can't sit on the Throne. He will come,* **117** *you are seated, & Christ in heavenly places only. Redeemed saints of. Lamb*

Jesus could no longer contain His excitement, and He interrupted her to say, "You have well said, 'I have no husband,' for you have had five husbands, and the one whom you now have is not your husband; in that you spoke truly."[15]

This was the high note of transparency and purity He was looking for. Now He had something He could work with. He began to talk to her about the living water. By the time He was done, she was ready to abandon her waterpots at the well. She ran back to the village to tell the people she had previously avoided all about the incredible Man at the well. She was so transformed that the same woman whom whole the village had rejected now led them back to Jacob's well to meet the Source of living water. *One conversation with the Master brought credibility to her–she had one worship encounter with Him, and the whole village listened.*

God Is Auditioning Hearts for the Celestial Choir

God is going to and fro in the earth right now, auditioning hearts to see who will become a true worshiper in His celestial choir. He isn't listening to the tonal quality of our voices or gauging our vocal ranges. Those things are unimportant to Him because His first concern is the song of the heart. Perhaps you are one of the many who are so desperate for an encounter with God that something inside you is pouring forth a passionate and hungry song of the heart. Can I tell you something? He is standing there right in front of you saying, "Keep singing. This is exactly what I've come for."

If you knew how close He is to you and how carefully He listens to every whispered amen and every crackle of your broken heart, you would be shocked. *The only thing the Father actively seeks is worshipers.* He loves and anoints the people whom most of us think are "important," like the preachers, worship leaders, and musicians, but what He really needs are worshipers. It makes me want to shout, "Come on Sister 'B,' *sing!*" Don't worry, He has placed His ear to your heart to see if you can hit that note. Can you?

Note from the heart to God's ear to y heart. He hears that note

"Father, we want an encounter with You that causes us to leave our waterpots at the well of man's religion. We want an encounter with You that we cannot get over. Turn our rejection into acceptance and our dusty, dry wells into inner spring experiences. We want to give You the best part—we give You worship and praise, adoration and thanksgiving in Jesus' name."

Go on, worshiper—worship! He's listening!

God is searching for worshipers this very moment. It is the only thing that brings Him from Heaven to earth. *It is the building material for His favorite house.* Remember that worship is for Him; it is His best and favorite part. Isn't it time for us to encircle the One we love with unceasing worship and adoration?

Endnotes

1. Sister "B" is a fictitious name for a very real and precious woman of God whom I will never forget.

2. Revelation 2:7.

3. James Strong, *Strong's Exhaustive Concordance of the Bible* (Peabody, MA: Hendrickson Publishers, n.d.), **Sychar** (#G1799).

4. This is the "Tenney version" of John 4:9.

5. John 4:10-11 NKJV.

6. John 4:21,23-24 NKJV.

7. I believe music will be *restored* to Heaven when it is populated with the redeemed saints who alone can sing "the song of the redeemed" before the Lamb (see Rev. 14:3). In the meantime, God wants to take His seat among us on earth as we enthrone Him on our praises and the song of the redeemed.

8. Luke 2:13-14.

9. Lucifer's ministry and ejection from Heaven are described in Isaiah 14:12-15.

10. Psalm 8:4 NKJV.

11. Matthew 21:16b NKJV.

12. See Revelation 15:2-3.

13. See Psalm 8:4-5; Ephesians 2:6; 2 Timothy 2:12.

14. See John 4:31-34.

15. John 4:17b-18 NKJV.

Chapter 9

Expanding the Throne Zone
On Earth As It Is in Heaven

Pastors around the country used to call me to "preach a revival" in their local churches, hoping I could help them raise excitement levels and perhaps win a few people to the Lord. All that ended the day my preaching career was ruined by a "hit and run," Jacob-at-Jabbok encounter with God.

The once respected evangelist they knew has been changed into a broken, weeping God chaser with a permanent limp and a perpetual hunger for more. I still burn to see the lost come to Jesus, but I am no longer interested in the kind of revival where people come to hear a man preach. I am in pursuit of the "Reviver"—when He comes to town, revival will come with Him!

God changed my "name" in an encounter that dislocated my denominational credentials and withered my dependence on my preaching gift so completely that, much of the time, all I can do is stand before a congregation and weep for His presence. It is hard to define what I am nowadays, so I basically coined the term, "God chaser," to describe it. But I can tell you what I'm after: *I am after a burning bush experience that triggers the release from slavery for everyone within the boundaries of His "throne zone."*

A friend of mine coined the term, "throne zone," to describe the atmosphere of worship that goes on around the throne of God. If somehow we can recreate the throne zone *on earth* as it is in Heaven in our churches and meetings, if our worship becomes so compelling that the manifest presence of God begins to put itself on display in our midst, then we will see the glory of God begin to flow through our cities. When this happens, the lost will come to Christ on a massive scale that we have never seen before. He said, "If I be lifted up, I will draw all men near."[1] We've concentrated on the "drawing" instead of the "lifting"! *Lift Jesus up.*

This statement is more than a teaching metaphor or a memorable preacher's phrase. It is a spiritual reality revealed in the prophet Ezekiel's vision thousands of years ago.[2] The prophet saw a river (signifying God's glory) flowing out from under the doors of His heavenly sanctuary and into the world, bringing life wherever it went. The depth of the river was shallowest at the sanctuary door, but it got deeper the further it flowed. Natural rivers are shallow at their headwaters or source, and they flow faster, deeper, and wider as they flow toward the sea. This is a picture of "the God-kind of revival."

What Happens When the Glory of God Falls on a City?

God is able to "do exceeding abundantly above all that we ask or think,"[3] and He wants to do something so big that it is beyond our ability to conceive of its magnitude or dimensions. He has moved upon men in the past, and He has moved upon our generation in a measure. I'm thankful for the way He has visited places like Toronto, Ontario; Pensacola, Florida; Houston, Texas; Baltimore, Maryland; and London, England. (There are countless other places in South America, Africa, Australia, Europe, and the Far East as well.) Yet I have to tell you that we have not yet seen what happens when the glory of God falls on a *city*. *We know what it looks like when God visits a church, but we've not yet seen what it looks like when He visits a city!*

A true revival should affect the city like the flood of glory in Ezekiel's vision affected Jerusalem and the nations. It has to happen in the Church first because we set the standard and the pace for what happens in a city. However, *what we see in our meetings should be nothing compared to His manifest power revealed in the streets! Acts 2 again, Lord!*

False Premises About Revival and Anointing Produce Misunderstanding

Sometimes we have false premises about revival and the people God uses in true revivals. These false premises about revival and the anointing can produce a lot of misunderstanding. Someone asked Duncan Campbell to define revival, and he touched on this in his reply:

> "First let me tell you what I mean by revival. An evangelistic campaign or a special meeting is not revival. In a successful evangelistic campaign or crusade, there will be hundreds, even thousands of people making decisions for Jesus Christ, but the community may remain untouched, and the churches continue much the same as before the outreach.
>
> "But in revival God moves in the region. Suddenly the community becomes God conscious, and the Spirit of God grips men and women in such a way that even work is given up as people give themselves to waiting upon God. In the midst of the Lewis Awakening [what we call the Hebrides revival], the parish minister...wrote, 'The Spirit of the Lord was resting wonderfully on the different townships of the region. His presence was in the homes of the people, on the meadow, and the moorland, and the public roads.'
>
> "This presence of God is the supreme characteristic of a God-sent revival. Of the hundreds who found Jesus Christ

during this time, fully 75 percent were saved before they came near a meeting, or heard a sermon by myself or any other minister in the parish. The power of God was moving in an operation that the fear of God gripped the souls of men before they ever reached the meetings."[4]

I will never be content merely to see the glory of God flow down the beautiful carpeted aisles of our churches. I want to see it flow down Main Street in an uncontrollable, unstoppable flood of glory that carries along everything in its path. I want His glory to invade the malls, grocery stores, health spas, and bars across town. I want to hear unchurched people say that they had to abandon an expensive entrée at their favorite restaurant to follow the dripping trail of God's glory to a church somewhere and demand, "Somebody tell me what to do!"

If good sermons and good songs were going to save the world, it would already be saved. There's a missing ingredient, and that "Divine Ingredient" is knocking at the door. The Hebrides revival provides a brief hint of what happens when glory breaks out. While describing the first days of the movement in the Hebrides Islands, Duncan Campbell remembered closing out a service in a crowded church and noticing that the congregation seemed reluctant to disperse. Many of the people just stood outside of the church building in a silence that was almost tense.

"Suddenly a cry is heard within, a young man burdened for the souls of his fellow men is pouring out his soul in intercession." Campbell said the man prayed until he collapsed and lay prostrate on the floor of the church building. He said, "The congregation, moved by a power they could not resist, came back into the church, and a wave of conviction swept over the gathering, moving strong men to cry to God for mercy."[5]

"God, You Promised!"

I asked an English friend about this incident, and it turns out he had heard Duncan Campbell speak about it. He told me, "Most of the people had already left the church according to

Mr. Campbell, but he said, 'The postman stood up and prayed, and then this young man stood up. I'll never forget the words he said: "Oh God, *You promised!*" All of a sudden it sounded like chariot wheels were rumbling on the roof of the church building. The next thing we knew, the church was filling back up again!' "

They learned later that many of the people had already started home when they suddenly felt the call to retrace their steps and return to the church building to pray. During some points of the Hebrides revival, Campbell said, "Most of them [the converts to Christ] only came to church to tell us that they had been converted because they would be weaving at a loom, or they would be plowing in the field when God would convict them. They just showed up to say, 'Where do I join, and what do I do?' "6

I am so tired of the manipulations of men supplanting the glory of God, thinking that the silly sermons they preach or the songs they sing is what causes anything! *He* is the root cause. *If we don't have a sovereign visitation of God, we are in trouble.* We must stop looking to man. Where are the young men (or the old, or the women!) who will stand in our midst, and say, "*God, You promised.*"

We need to stop looking to the platform for the power of God. We have put enormous pressure on the servants of God to try to manipulate and create what can only come from God. We need to wait on Him and seek Him until something breaks in the heavens!

The Voice of Prayer Mingled With the Groans of the Repentant

According to Duncan Campbell, this divine visitation just continued. They tasted a measure of divine habitation that rocked the region. "One evening, as the congregation was leaving the church and moving down toward the main road, the Spirit of God fell on the people in a Pentecostal power, no other word can describe it. In a few minutes the awareness of *the presence of the Most High* became so wonderful and so subduing, that one could only say with Jacob of old, 'Surely the Lord is in this place.' And there under the open heavens, and by the roadside, the voice of prayer was mingled with the groans of the repentant as free grace awoke men with light from on high.

"Soon the whole island was in the grip of a mighty movement of the Spirit, bringing deep conviction of sin and a hunger for God. This movement was different than the other islands, and that while in Lewis [island] there were physical manifestations and prostrations, there were not here, but the work was as deep, and the result was enduring."[7] This is a picture, a foretaste, of God's will for the Church today.

It is up to the Church to birth the purposes of God in this generation. During the years I pastored a church, I used to tell couples expecting their first baby, "I need to tell you that when your baby is born, your whole life will change." Their typical answer was sort of a nod and a smile, "Yeah, yeah, we understand." I wanted to just take them by the shoulders and look them in the eye and say once more, "No, no, you don't understand! In fact, you don't even have a clue. You think you do but you really don't."

We Don't Have a Clue

Too many of us sit together in our "revival" meetings and nod and smile and say, "Yeah, we know what revival is, and we are ready for it." The truth is that we don't have a clue. The original purpose of the Church was to be a meeting place between God and man, not a glorified "bless me club" or a receiving place where man comes solely to receive from God. Church was not created as a spiritual bless-me-trough where we can roll in the anointing and pig out. Church was created for you to give something of yourself to Him.

If we want to restore the Church to its original power, we must return to God's original recipe for revival in Second Chronicles 7:14: "If My people who are called by My name will humble themselves, and pray...."[8] The next phrase reveals the step that goes *beyond prayer*. God says, *"and seek My face."* We think we know everything there is to know about prayer. We say we understand prayer, and we recite prayers, we can even prevail in prayer. Yet I wonder how many of us fully understand God's command in Second Chronicles to *seek His face*? We must seek the face of God, not His hand. *Prayer is petitioning–"seeking His face" is positioning*.

We must abandon the entertainment-based worship that tickles our ears and encourages our selfish desires to constantly hear something, feel something, or do something that makes us feel good. Aren't you hungry for *more*? Someday, somewhere, we will meet to seek His face and the glory of God will settle down among us. When that happens, we won't leave that place with just a temporary touch of God's anointing. Everyone who sees His glory will leave dramatically different than before He came.

Picture the Glory of God
Riveting Entire Communities

We need mass Damascus Road experiences, where the glory of God is revealed to an entire assembly of people all at once. In a moment of time, God's manifest presence transformed Saul of Tarsus from a persecutor into a propagator of the gospel. Now picture the glory of God riveting entire communities with conviction after engulfing them in the light of His glory!

This is the way to win the lost. If worship is done right, then soul-winning and altar calls don't take a whole lot of words. Simply say, "Come," and they will. Why? Worship brings God's presence, and His presence drives away everything else. That means people in the *throne zone* may be given for the

THE COMING REVIVAL IS NOT ABOUT SERMONS AND INFORMATION; IT'S GOING TO BE ABOUT WORSHIP AND IMPARTATION.

first time the opportunity of an unfettered choice when His presence comes.

The coming revival is not going to be about *sermons and information*; it's going to be about *worship and impartation*. The preaching of the Word won't stop, but the sermons that come will serve the same purpose as Peter's impromptu sermon on the Day of Pentecost. They won't necessarily *produce* desired actions in people; they will come after the fact to *explain* what happened after "God came down." (Right now, we tend to preach by faith before the fact and *hope* it will happen.) Worship draws down the presence of God.

The "Suddenly of God" Requires the "Waiting of Man"

"Suddenly" there came an upper room experience where He threw open the windows of Heaven and rushed down. That's what we want: the rushing in of God, that suddenly of God. *But you don't have the "suddenly of God" without the "waiting of man."* We need to go after the face of God. We can no longer be content with God's just slipping His hand out from under the veil to dispense gospel goodies to us anymore. We want the veil to open, and we want to pass through into the Holy of Holies to have a life-changing encounter with Him. Then we need to prop open that veil with Davidic passion and worship so the glory of God will manifest itself in the streets of the city.

The Church is pregnant with God's purposes. Our body feels swollen; our belly is distended. We don't know when or where the baby will be born, but we know a baby is about to be born, and we are desperate. To be honest, I hope you live with so much holy frustration that you can't sleep tonight. I pray that a gnawing hunger for the presence of God rises up in your heart with devastating results. I want you to be "ruined" for everything except His purposes.

On the day the Church rises up to build a mercy seat according to the pattern of Heaven, God will wave good-bye to Michael and Gabriel and will literally set up a throne zone in our midst! Let me assure you that when the glory of God shows up like that, we won't have to advertise or promote anything. Once the Bread of Heaven takes His seat among us, the hungry will come.

> **"Father, we fan the flames of hunger.**
> **May we never be the same. Set our hearts on fire."**

There is only one way you and I can pay the price of obedience to create a throne zone on earth. We need to let our hearts be so broken before Him that the things that break His heart also break our hearts.

Put your hand on your heart and, if you dare, pray this prayer:

> *"Break my heart, Lord;*
> *I don't want to be the same.*
> *Soften my heart, Lord Jesus,*
> *and let me dwell in Your presence."*

The Fail-Safe Way to Open Heaven's Gates

There is one fail-safe way to open the gates of Heaven and close the gates of hell on the ruling principalities and powers of darkness in your region. Pray, repent, intercede, and worship God until you break open a hole in the heavens and God flips on His glory light switch. Satanic forces will flee in every direction!

Even our best "spiritual warfare" and our loudest screams against demonic forces can't compare with the power released when God turns on the light of His glory. The status quo isn't working. We can't get the world into our church buildings—our lifestyles have convinced people that we don't have anything to offer them. We must get the "God of the Church" to them.

It is up to us. We can remain satisfied with our bland diets of powerless services interspersed with a few "good" services each year, or we can pursue God at any cost. Most of us are uncomfortable with change, but change is a part of what God is about to do. He is redefining the Church and making our religious labels totally obsolete. I can tell you this much about it: *His manifest presence is going to be supreme.* That means it won't really matter who speaks, who sings, who prays, or who does anything in those services—*as long as He is there.*

Caught in an Outbreak of His Presence!

People don't understand what it means to be caught in an outbreak of the manifest presence of God. Duncan Campbell described an incident in the Hebrides that was burned into his memory.

"At my request several officers from the parish visited the island, bringing with them a young lad who recently was brought to the saving knowledge. After spending time and prayer at the cottage, we went to the church to find it crowded now. But seldom did I experience such bondage of spirit, and preaching was most difficult, so much so that when only half way through my address I stopped preaching.

"Just then my eye caught sight of this young lad who was visibly moved, and appeared to be deeply burdened. Leaning over the pulpit I said, 'Donald, will you lead us in prayer.' There was an immediate response, and in that moment the flood gates of heaven opened, and the congregation was struck as by a hurricane, and many cried out for mercy.

"But the most remarkable feature of this visitation was not what happened there in the church, but the spiritual impact on the island. Men, who until that moment had no thought of seeking after God, were suddenly arrested where they stood, sat or laid, and became deeply concerned about their soul, until they said, This is the Lord's doing."[9]

I Want the Heavens to Break Over Entire Cities

I'm sick of reading from the menu of programmed revival. I want the heavens to break open over *entire cities*, but the

Church knows very little about this type of evangelism. Our specialty seems to be "program evangelism." We know how to make phone calls, mail letters, and knock on doors in an organized way to win souls to Christ, and I'm thankful for every soul that has come to Christ through these methods.

We also know about "power evangelism," the method of soul winning introduced to American churches nearly 20 years ago by the late John Wimber. This is also a program, but it mixes the healing anointing with organized evangelism outreach.

We must learn how to attract God to the Church in such a way that He can manifest His glory freely. When that happens, we won't have to worry about attracting men. God will do it Himself. "Presence" evangelism occurs when Jesus is lifted up in all His glory, because He promised that *He* will draw all men to Himself.[10] When *we* take on the responsibility of attracting people to the church, all we get is a crowd.

We try to attract man, thinking that's our job.
When are we going to learn?
The primary purpose of the Church is to attract Him!

The bottom line is simply this: *We need more of God and less of man.* We need people who will pray until the heavens collapse, crying out, *"God, You promised!"*

You may be right at the door to the throne zone this very moment. God wants to meet you where you are. You can leave this divine appointment with an impartation from God that can bring revival to your church and city and bring the prodigals home in your family. But no one can do it for you. You must personally walk through that door of death called repentance. The glory of God is waiting just on the other side, but *only dead men can see His face.* Only beaten worshipers can build the mercy seat through their broken, purified, and repentant worship. It is just possible that you might be the "somebody" who will change the destiny of a nation.

When people asked John Wesley how he drew such large crowds and led so many people to Christ, he told them, "I just set myself on fire for God and people come to see me burn." Somebody has to start the fire. If not you, then who? If not here and now, then where and when? Just remember that you have no right to pray for *the fire of God* unless you are willing to be *the fuel of God!*

I Couldn't Run Anymore!

Miraculous things happen when God's glory begins to settle down over a place. I know of a church in Georgia where an outbreak of God began to invade the community outside the church building. The testimony of one woman illustrates in a trickle what I'm praying for in a torrent. She told me:

"Three Sundays ago I was sitting in my living room about a half mile away from the church. I didn't know what it was, but a spirit, a presence of God entered my living room. I was sitting there smoking a Marlboro cigarette, drinking Bud Light, and channel surfing when the presence of God just came into my living room. I ran from it at first. In fact, I got up and moved into the kitchen.

"The first week I could go from the kitchen to the living room. The presence was only in the living room, not the kitchen. Last week, it not only came in the living room, but it invaded the kitchen, so I went to my bedroom.

"This morning when I got up, it had pushed all the way into my bedroom and *I couldn't run anymore!* I knew it was coming from here, and I just had to come."

That woman was saved that night, and her testimony perfectly illustrates the way "presence evangelism" invades a city. If you take her testimony and multiply it by hundreds, thousands, and millions of lives, you might have a glimpse of what God has in store for this generation if we can create a throne zone of His presence that just keeps pushing through the city. When that happens, people won't be able to run anymore because mercy and grace will be flowing through the streets of the city. This river of glory will only get wider and deepe. ure further it goes. God, do it!

*"Father, impart to us a broken heart, as Your heart was broken, and let beaten winged worshipers build a place of habitation. We turn our back on what is good to seek what is best. We want Your **kabod**, Your glory, O God. Father, thank You for the anointing and for what it does. But it still smells like man. We pray, 'Let man die, and let the glory of God come.' "*

Somebody needs to pray the prayer of Moses, "Show me Your glory!" We need the glory of God in our churches, homes, and public schools. I look for the day some young person will bow his or her head to pray in the public school lunchroom and the glory of God suddenly fall on the entire school! We've had the blood of students flow in the hallways—it's time for the blood of Jesus to flow in the schools!

He Will Only Come Through the Cracks of Our Brokenness

We need God in our midst. If we build the mercy seat, He will come. If we want God to show up in our churches, He will only come through the cracks of our brokenness, not through the wholeness of our arrogance. *Only broken earthly vessels can hold the heavenly glory.* It doesn't make sense, but it is true.

I can't pray anything upon you except my hunger. I am hungry for God, and He promised us that He would meet that need: "Blessed are they which do hunger and thirst...for they shall be filled."[11] The glory cannot come to a full vessel. We must cry out for more of Him and less of us. We must empty our cups of "self" before He can fill them up with Himself. It is the only way to open the heavens and release the glory of God over our cities.

Can you imagine what will happen if we empty ourselves and His manifest presence comes? What will happen when God's manifest presence settles over a church in a city? We must create a throne zone and expand the parameters of the

veil
walk a gate or door

manifest presence of God where His glory is made available to everyone without a veil, a wall, or a gate.

When there is no barrier between God and man, you will hear Him if He whispers. It won't take a hurricane-force wind of God to move you; rather it will be just the gentlest zephyr, the smallest breeze, the lightest whisper from His heart. If we can create such a place through our repentant "beaten" worship, God will come. David's tabernacle was His "favorite house" because of its unveiled worship of intimacy. It is this atmosphere of intimacy that creates a place of divine habitation—a "throne zone" on earth as in Heaven—God's favorite house.

Jesus, let Your glory flow, let it flow. We seek Your face.

Endnotes

1. See John 12:32.
2. I also discussed this timely passage from Ezekiel 47 in *The God Chasers* (Shippensburg, PA: Destiny Image Publishers, 1998), 106-107.
3. Ephesians 3:20.
4. Duncan Campbell, from conversations with Alan Vincent. These remarks by Duncan Campbell are available on audiotapes from the GodChasers.network at P.O. Box 3355, Pineville, Louisiana 71361, or from the website, www.GodChasers.net.
5. Ibid.
6. Ibid.
7. Ibid.
8. NKJV.
9. Campbell, from conversations with Alan Vincent.
10. See John 12:32.
11. Matthew 5:6.

Chapter 10

Discover the Secret Power of a Doorkeeper
(In the Right Place)

Ayoung man who interviewed six elderly prayer veterans of the New Hebrides revival said, "One of them looked at me with fire in his ancient eyes, and he said in a broken brogue, *'If you ever find Him, never, never, never, never let go!'*" The experiences and insights that these men shared with their young interviewer were recorded for posterity on an audiotape that I have in my possession. I just can't get over those words, "If you ever find Him, never, never, never, never let go!"[1]

What do these words mean? They mean that if you manage to get the door of Heaven propped open, don't ever let it close again. You might be left at a useless door of the past, guarding only the fragrance of what used to be. Now you will find yourself running through the streets like the bride of Solomon, desperately asking other people, "Have you see Him? His head and hair are white like wool. I didn't know it was Him; I was too tired when He knocked."

Desperate God chasers are being graced to "catch Him" in divine visitation more than ever, and there is heavenly purpose in it all. Every day I hear more reports of people stumbling on their knees through doors or gates in time that let them peek into eternity. The same thing happened to Jacob when he went to sleep too close to a gate between the heavens. He awoke with a clear vision of an open Heaven before him, and it marked the beginning of a permanent change in his life.

IF YOU GET THE DOOR OF HEAVEN PROPPED OPEN, DON'T EVER LET IT CLOSE AGAIN!

When we find ourselves in places of divine visitation, it is like a seam in time has opened up before us. When Eternity Himself enters our little playhouse in the land of time, everything of earthly importance seems to fade away. Why? *Because God is in the house.* Eternity has visited our little time-bound world, and His glory is filling up our cramped room. That is why three hours seem like a mere three minutes when we get lost in His presence in the midst of our worship. In those moments, we have come closest to the gate. We can almost slip the surly bonds of time into the timeless realm of eternity.

Be Careful Not to Lose the Place of Divine Access

When Jacob stumbled across the gate of Heaven, he set up stones to mark the place and said, "I don't want to forget this." However, if we are not careful, we can use markers from this realm that don't fit the markers in the spirit realm.

Most people try to mark the "location" of their spiritual experiences with temporal, ever-changing markers. They may tell the worship leader, "Let's sing that song we sang three weeks ago, because we were singing it when I had a visitation of God." *Unfortunately, temporal markers can never mark a place of eternity.* That's why they come back to the worship leader and say, "Well, it's good, but it's not the same." The problem is they set up the wrong kind of marker. *They should have marked the position and hunger of their hearts, not the song.*

One time my grandfather took me to his favorite fishing spot. After he had carefully maneuvered the boat into just the right spot, he said, "Now, son, if you'll always fish at this little spot right here, you'll catch a lot of fish. Right here you are over a submerged outcropping."

I went back there later on and positioned my boat in the same area, but I didn't catch anything. When I got home, I called my grandfather and said, "Big Daddy, there weren't any fish there."

He said, "No, son, there's always fish there. You just weren't right on it."

"Well, I couldn't have been very far...."

"You don't understand, son," he said. "You don't have to be 50 feet away to miss the spot. You could be just two feet away from the right spot and still not catch any fish. You have to be right over it. Come on, I'll go with you this time."

We went back to Big Daddy's fishing spot once more and he said, "Now, you drive the boat and get it positioned." So I maneuvered the boat until I had it right where I thought it was supposed to be, and then I looked over at Big Daddy. He just smiled and said, "Son, you're not at the right spot—*it's over there.*"

These Are the Wrong Kinds of Markers

Whenever fishermen come across a good "fishin' hole," they have an urge to mark that spot for future fishing trips. The problem is that it's hard to mark a place that's underwater. Some people try to do it with a sealed milk jug and a weight, but most of the time the wind and the water blows these temporary markers out of position, or a speed boat cuts the line. These are the wrong kinds of markers. Big Daddy knew how to get back to his special spot because he used permanent landmarks that wouldn't change when the wind blew. He explained to me, "You have to look up on the horizon." Then he said,

"Do you see that tree over there?" Once he gave me the proper landmarks, I could correctly position the boat. He said, "Now, that special spot is right here," and sure enough, it was.

Don't try to use temporal or temporary earthly markers to mark places of heavenly access, because they don't always work. Jacob set up stones to mark his nighttime encounter with God. Many years later, when the Israelites finally crossed the Jordan River into the Promised Land, they marked their crossing with stones. Since the riverbed was dry where they crossed, they took their marker stones from the middle of Jordan's riverbed and set them up on shore. Now those stones made good markers because stones from a riverbed have been worn smooth by the action of the water, while stones that are not from a river are rough and jagged.

Every time their children passed by that pile of smooth stones, it was clear to them that those stones were out of place. They marked a *split seam* of eternity in the veil of time. When they said, "Those rocks don't belong here," their parents would say, "You're right, son. Those rocks are from the time of His visitation." *Those markers reminded generation after generation of Israelites about the day the river parted because the heavens opened.*

I Would Rather Be a Doorkeeper...

God chasers need a different kind of "marker" to mark the places where the heavens have opened. What can we use—a favorite "revival song list" or a special "revival wardrobe"? None of these will work. Once again we need to turn to the Word of God and take a page out of David's intimate journey with God. David said, "For a day in Your courts is better than a thousand. I would rather be a doorkeeper in the house of my God than dwell in the tents of wickedness."[2]

Why did he say that? "David, you are a king. That is a real position of influence. Why would you want to be a doorkeeper?" David was saying, "No, I've learned something: A doorkeeper *at the right door* has more influence in the world than a king on his throne! A doorkeeper in the house of God is a doorkeeper at *the gate of Heaven*. Now if I can just find that opening in Heaven...."

The glory of God is pent up in Heaven like floodwaters behind a dam, and God has openly declared His intention to flood the whole world with the knowledge of His glory. Most of the time we don't really know where the door is or how to go through the door once we stumble across it for the first time.

Our solution to the problem is to forget the best, which is represented by a flood of God's glory. Instead of waiting patiently upon the Lord, we present the "good" (the *anointing*) God has given us as if it were the "best" (God's *manifest glory*). This happens when we claim, "God is here!" implying His glory has come down when it really hasn't.

Paul told us, "For now we see through a glass, darkly."[3] That could be our theme Scripture. We have made a way of life out of the second-best. We bring people one by one to look through our "peephole of the anointing" just to let them know there is something on the other side. Then we frustrate the world when we say *"We've lost the key to opening the door, though."*

We busied ourselves teaching people how to be satisfied with somebody's laying hands on them, and we never told them that God's anointing on flesh is at best a cheap substitute for the manifest presence of God Himself coming down among them. Listen, if God shows up, you won't need me or anyone else to lay hands on you, I promise you. Seek the Anointer, not the anointed or even the anointing. *There is a vast difference between my hands on your head and His finger writing on the fleshly walls of your heart!*

Who Will Find the Ancient Keys That Jingled in God's Hand?

The thing God promised is going to happen, and a flood of God's glory is going to come. It is going to start somewhere with someone, but where? Who will find the ancient keys that jingled in the hands of God when He told Peter, "Here are the keys to the Kingdom. Whatever you open on earth will be opened in Heaven"?[4] Who will hear a knock at the other side and slip that ancient key into that door to open the gate of Heaven? Wherever it happens, whoever opens that door, the result will be an unstoppable, immeasurable flood of the glory of God. If the glory of God is going to cover the earth, it has to start somewhere. Why not here? Why not you?

There are some Kingdom keys lying around, and somebody has to find them and prop the door open. God said, "I sought for a man among them who would make a wall, and stand in the gap before Me on behalf of the land, that I should not destroy it; but I found no one."[5] We need to strip away our overly religious ways of looking at things to really understand what God is saying. Where and what is this "gap" that God wants us to fill?

On one occasion, I took my entire family to Atlanta, Georgia, so they could be with me while I spoke at a church in that city. When departure time came, everyone filed out of the hotel room and headed for the elevator. Everyone had their hands full of bags, suitcases, and packages, including my youngest daughter. It seems like she has her own little family of stuffed animal figures called "Beanie Babies," and on this occasion she had brought the entire "family" along in her over-stuffed backpack.

The Door Started Closing...

Have you ever seen little children trying to carry more than they can handle? Andrea was dragging her backpack down the hallway and lagging behind a little bit. The elevator in that particular hotel closed really quickly, and just as Andrea began to step onto the elevator, the door started closing on her. Everyone else was already on the elevator.

Andrea instinctively backed out of the elevator as quickly as she could, and that was when I saw a look of panic flood her face. I could imagine what was going through her mind in that moment: *Dear God, they are going to leave me here! I'll be stuck up here all by myself in this hotel while they drive away without me.*

My fatherly instincts also kicked in when the door started to close. I quickly thrust my hand between the elevator doors and hoped I would be able to force them back open. I finally got it open, but I literally had to force my hands between the doors and physically push them apart. Once I pried open the doors, I stepped between them and held them open. In that moment, I saw a look of sheer relief on Andrea's face, and she said, "My Daddy is ho'ding it open for me." With a sheepish grin and a little girl giggle, she snuck in between those doors and felt safe once again.

God never intended for us to use our favorite hymns or worship songs to mark our divine encounters or to hold open the gates of Heaven. A sermon won't do it; nor will a sparkling personality or a powerful healing ministry do it. God has a better idea. *Prop open that gate with your own life!* Become a doorkeeper and open the door to let the light of Heaven shine on your church and city.

Nothing Beats a Living, Serving Doorkeeper

Sometimes I think our national restaurant chains are more sensitive than we are! I like to go to a particular restaurant chain that specializes in Italian food, partly because I like the food and partly because I like their service. I've noticed that this restaurant thinks so much of its customers that it positions a doorkeeper at the door to personally greet every customer when they come in. In other places they may prop open the door with a plastic doorstop or let the door slam shut. *Nothing beats a living, serving doorkeeper when it comes to ushering in guests and meeting needs.*

Let me ask you this: *What is the purpose of the Church?* It isn't meant to serve only you or me. The Church is for Him above all. Now if we have an encounter with Him, if we somehow thrust our hands through the veil into the open heaven, it is our responsibility to hold open the gates of Heaven for the benefit of those who follow behind us.

If you stumble through that door in the midst of your repentant, beaten worship, then position yourself in the doorway and prop it open. *Stand in the gap.* God has promised He will help rebuild His favorite house, if we can hold the door open. If you can imagine yourself holding open a large overhead door with your hands, then you have a picture of a gatekeeper in the right place—*propping open the door to God's presence with upraised hands in the posture and position of praise and worship.*

David Entertained God's Presence Continually for 36 Years!

David discovered a key that we need to rediscover in our day. He did more than return God's presence to Jerusalem. He did more than display God's glory in an open tent without walls or a veil of separation. Somehow he managed to *entertain God's presence in his humble tent and keep an open heaven over all Israel for almost 36 years!* David's generation benefited from his worship.

When we open the windows of Heaven through our worship, we also need to post a guard—a doorkeeper—inside the dimension of God (worship) to hold open the windows of Heaven. In David's day, the Levitical worshipers surrounded the ark of the covenant with continuous worship and praise. *They enjoyed the benefits of a continuously open heaven because somebody stood in the gate and held it open.* If you are a pastor or church leader, your primary responsibility in your city is to be a gatekeeper. You have the opportunity to succeed or fail in your given responsibility. *Be a gate keeper*

A gatekeeper can be anyone who has the responsibility of opening the windows of Heaven to a city. They could be church leaders, intercessors, and every worshiper. An open heaven refers to the free access of God's presence to man and to the free flow of God's glory to man's dimension, with as little demonic hindrance as possible.

Lot was a gatekeeper in Sodom and Gomorrah. We know this because the Bible says Lot "sat in the gate of Sodom."[6] Despite his poor choice of cities, he clearly recognized righteousness

make me a gate keeper

when he encountered it in his angelic visitors. He specifically "opened the gates" to righteousness and welcomed his holy visitors into his home. Lot also recognized unrighteousness for what it was, but he failed to "close the gates" to the sin that was consuming his city. Because Lot didn't take the proper stand and have an effect on the city, Sodom and Gomorrah had an effect on him. In the end, *Sodom was destroyed by fire because God's gatekeeper didn't do his job.* Office

David also was a gatekeeper, but he understood the importance of his office. When he penned Psalm 84:10, I feel that he was saying, "I would rather be a doorkeeper at the right door, because that is the place of *real* influence." *Never underestimate the power of God's presence.* If you can be a doorkeeper and open the door of the manifest presence of God to your church and your community, understand that you have been placed in the most influential position in the entire world. Like the Levites of old, we are all called to be a gatekeeper people, the people of His presence. You can literally become a walking doorway to God's presence. People can sense the glory light shining under the door.

The man named Obededom discovered the importance of being a doorkeeper in the right place. Most believe that he was a part of the Levitical order, but we do know this much for sure about him: *He knew what it was like to have God dwell in his house instead of merely visit there.* God to Dwell in this House

He Knew What to Do When
Visitation Turns to Habitation

Obededom knew what to do when divine visitation turned into divine habitation, and he discovered there were side benefits that came with the job. His crops grew better, his dog stopped biting people, his roof didn't leak, his kids didn't get sick, and everything in his life was incredibly blessed. You know something good is going on when your crops are so blessed that, in three months time, everybody knows about it. Finally the word reached all the way to King David in Jerusalem:

"David, you won't believe it: Obededom has turned into a millionaire in three months."

David said, "I knew I had it right. I've got to get that ark to Jerusalem.[7] If Obededom can be that blessed locally, then if I can put the ark in its proper place, we will all be blessed nationally."

Just how much was Israel blessed when David maintained the tabernacle all those years? Even though we haven't begun to worship and serve as we should, if the Church and its worship were withdrawn from the world today, things would spiral down very quickly. On the other hand, if the people of God can ever put the glory of God back in the Church in its proper place, the entire nation can be blessed.

You Will Find Him Wherever the Ark Went

No matter where the ark went in David's reign as king, you will find a certain man following it. His name is mentioned six times in First Chronicles 15 and 16. This is what happened according to Tenney's version:

Knock, knock.

King David:	"Obed, this is King David. You know that ark we left here about three months ago? We're here to pick it up now. My, but everything looks nice around here, Obed."
Obed:	"King David, let me get this straight: You are going to take the ark away from me?"
King David:	"Yes, well, as I recall, you were a little bit afraid when we left it here."
Obed:	"That was then. Now I've learned that wherever that ark is, there is blessing."
King David:	"Well, we need to take it now because I've prepared a special place for the ark in Jerusalem. It will take us a while to get it

	there, but once we do, the *whole nation* will be blessed."
Obed:	"King David, could you hold on just a minute?...Mom, you and the kids pack up! Yeah, pack up all your stuff and gather all the clothes."
Obed, Jr.:	"Where are we going, Dad?"
Obed:	*"Wherever this ark is going, that's where we're going."*

The next time we hear about Obededom, do you know what it says he's doing? *The Bible says he was a doorkeeper for the ark!*[8] Obededom moved when the ark moved. It almost looks like he took on every job he could just to be near the presence of the Lord. In one verse Obededom is described as a porter, which means he must have said, "I'll help carry the thing."[9] I believe that when they asked him why, Obededom said, "Because I just want to be wherever the ark is. I want to be a gatekeeper, a doorkeeper. Honestly, I want to hold the door open because I found out about the blessing...."

One time I was preaching in an extremely hot location in the tropics. There was no air conditioning in the building, so I asked the local sponsors, "Would you set the podium right by that door? There's a strong breeze coming through the doorway. I'm going to be preaching, and I want to try to stay cool."

The whole time I preached, I could feel the wind constantly blowing through my legs and whistling past my arms. Since I was in the right place, the tropical heat wasn't so bad. Let me tell you there is a benefit to standing in the doorway to Heaven. When you become a doorkeeper and prop open the door of Heaven, you can feel the rushing of the mighty wind of the Holy Spirit as it fills the place of meeting with glory.

No wonder the 120 were drunk on the Day of Pentecost. They had broken open the heavens, and they stood in the doorway as the rushing mighty wind of God exploded from Heaven and filled their earthly house. His glory then spilled out into the street, and the next time you read about it God's Word says, "All of Jerusalem was filled with their doctrine."[10] Then we read that "...all who dwelt in Asia heard the word."[11]

What happened? *Somebody found the door and just propped it open with their own lives.* The side benefit is that gatekeepers get to have an encounter with God too, even as His presence flows to the nations. This is the blessing and heritage of a gatekeeper *in the right place.*

We Need Doorkeepers More Than Kings or Presidents

Where are the doorkeepers? God knows we need doorkeepers more than we need kings and presidents. We need people who know how to access His presence and open the door for the glory of God to come into our homes, churches, cities, and nations. David again writes the vision so we can run:

> *Lift up your heads, O you **gates**! And be lifted up, **you everlasting doors**! And the King of glory shall come in.*[12]

Gates don't have heads. It is obvious that *we* are the gates in this Psalm. If we lift up our heads, what happens? The Hebrew literalization of that phrase is "be *opened* up you everlasting doors." When we obey this command, the King of glory Himself will come in. What does all this mean? We, as the Church, are literally the gateway for the rest of the world to have an encounter with God. *When you stand in the place of worship, you are literally opening up and swinging wide a spiritual gate, an entrance for the risen Lord.* A modern-day David named Martin Smith sings a new song based on an ancient theme:

"Fling wide your heavenly gates.
Prepare the way of the risen Lord..."

This call to worship must be the anthem of the Church.

If I Can Just Get My Hands in That Crack

We are called to take our place beside our great High Priest and stand in the gap between the world who doesn't know and those who do. We are holding open the rapidly closing "elevator" that takes people to Heaven. Sometimes I can sense a crack in the heavenlies even as I preach messages to congregations in certain places, where it seems like the heavens are about to open. I sometimes think to myself, *If I can just get my hands in that crack and pry it or pray it open, maybe the glory of God will come down tonight.*

Gatekeepers are rare and priceless in God's economy. Perhaps David peered into the darkness of the night one evening and felt reassured when he saw the dancing feet and outstretched arms of the late-shift worship team filtering the glory of God and was inspired to write,

> *Behold, bless the Lord, all you servants of the Lord, who by night stand in the house of the Lord! Lift up your hands in the sanctuary, and bless the Lord.*[13]

If we ever want to move from a visitation of God to a habitation of God, someone has to learn how to hold open the door to the heavenlies. It appears that some of us would prefer to go inside the veil and let the door swing shut behind us. We don't care about the world as long as we get in. I'm sorry, maybe it is because of the Southern culture in which I was raised, but I was taught to be a gentleman. You don't just walk through a door and let it shut behind you. You hold it open for others. I think it is time for the Church to pick up some spiritual etiquette and say, "Let's hold open the door of Heaven." Then those who watch us from afar can say, "Bless the Lord, all you servants of the Lord, who by night stand in the house of the Lord"—*propping open the heavens.*

How long have you been praying for an open heaven over your church and community? I promise you it is *not nearly as long as He has been waiting behind the door for it to open.* In the Song of Solomon, we see Him pictured as the loving groom, peering through the latticework for some glimpse of His beloved. He is waiting behind the door saying, "If I can ever get

My Church into position, then I can throw open the windows and gates of Heaven and pour out...."

Our Inactivity Can Open Hell and Close Heaven

Who needs to get in position? *The gatekeepers*. God is looking for people who have the keys to the Kingdom and know how to use them (that's you and me!). The sad part of it all is that not only can our obedient activity in praise and worship open Heaven and close hell, but *our inactivity can just as effectively open hell and close Heaven*. Jesus rebuked the religious leaders of His day, telling the Pharisees,

> *Woe to you lawyers! For you have taken away the **key** of knowledge. You did not enter in yourselves, and **those who were entering in you hindered**.*[14]

This warning is so strong that every one of us must ask ourselves: "Have I been an impediment or a hindrance to God's Kingdom by being locked into something God never said or ordained?" Perhaps the greatest problem in the Church preventing the opening of the heavens today is the fear of man. It permeates pastoral leadership, and some leaders admit that the fear of man drives 90 percent of their decisions. *Man-oriented and man-pleasing decisions are driving the Church toward spiritual bankruptcy* and are closing the windows of Heaven. We must make up our minds that we are after only one thing: **We want God**. We want to open the windows of Heaven so His glory will flood our churches, our cities, and the lives of our people.

The only time God will break down the gates the enemy has erected in the earth is when Jesus comes back the next time. On that great day, the Eastern Gate is just going to open before Him. Until then, we control whether or not He comes to our city. Are you willing to weep over your city like Jesus wept over Jerusalem?

Prop Open the Door So the King of Glory Can Come In

You have the keys in your hand, transferred by the Spirit through the leadership of the Church since Jesus first delivered them into Peter's hands. Are you going to unlock the windows of Heaven and lock up the gates of hell? Will you prop open the door so the King of Glory can personally come in to *rebuild His favorite house,* **the house that worship built?**

In the meantime, God is peeping out through the mini-blinds of Heaven and saying, "I want to throw open the window. I want to do away with the veil. I've hated veils from the beginning, so I rip them every time I get a chance. If I can get the Church to take its place as repentant worshipers around the throne, I will throw open the windows of Heaven. *Judgment will stop with My worshipers, but My mercy will slip through to the pagans and heathens looking in at the Church.*" They won't even see the worshipers because their backs are turned to the world. All they will see is the blue flame of the *shekinah* glory of God. And the lost will say, "That's mercy." That's the mercy seat.

God is still hiding from the world because He cannot flow through the streets until the Church takes its place and begins to filter the glory. So the hunting eyes of God are darting to and fro while He asks, "Where is somebody who will be a go-between, who will stand in the gap and make up the hedge? Don't let it fall. Hold it high for other places and other people. I'm looking for somebody who can prop open the windows of Heaven in the weeping zone."

We Must Let Our Uzzahs Die
So the Glory Can Be Restored

With this revelation there comes responsibility. Don't expect to go about business as usual because you now know where the Church is supposed to stand. It is okay to be seeker-friendly, but our first calling is to be Spirit-friendly. *Seeker-friendly is fine, but Spirit-friendly is fire!* We must let our Uzzahs die so the glory can be restored to God as we reach for Heaven with one hand and the earth with the other.

Can you feel the wind and the breeze of the Spirit whipping between your legs? When God shows up in your services, it is better than having billboards around town. Services like that do more than any TV advertisement. Why? Because it doesn't attract man; it attracts God. If you get God, then you don't have to worry about man. The hungry will come.

If you can just learn how to stand in a place like that, you will begin to feel surrounded by His presence. As you begin to walk in it, your life becomes a walking window of His presence that is subject to being opened at any time by soul-hungry men. That means that the glory of God could break out every time you visit a grocery store or a convenience store.

Something is shaking the Church. We hit a bump, our new cart was shaken, and our Uzzahs are dying or dead. We want Him, but we've had to learn the right ways to welcome and reverence His presence. Our shaking hands have found the rip in the veil. We've found the door of Heaven, and God is looking for a place of habitation. Throw open the veil and keep it open. *One good service is not enough.*

Turn Your Focus Away
From the Bleating Complaints of Men

Will the doorkeepers rise up and take their positions at the right door? Will the repentant, beaten worshipers turn their focus away from the bleating complaints of men to offer the sweet incense of praise to enthrone the Great King? If they do...if *we* do, *then He will come.* And He will build again the tabernacle of David, His house of unending, unveiled worship among redeemed men. Then the gates of Heaven will be opened and flood the Church, the cities, and the whole earth with the knowledge of His glory and draw all men unto Himself.

I think I see Him gathering the components to rebuild His favorite house...

Worshipers.
Broken in this world, just right for that world.
Are you one?

Here, help me. That's it—stand right there.
Lift up your hands...there you go.
Worship.

Endnotes

1. I have made this tape available to the public through my ministry for just the cost of the tape plus shipping and handling. Contact GodChasers.network at P.O. Box 3355, Pineville, Louisiana 71361, or call (318) 442-4273. You may also visit our website at www.GodChasers.net.
2. Psalm 84:10 NKJV.
3. 1 Corinthians 13:12.
4. See Matthew 16:19.
5. Ezekiel 22:30 NKJV.
6. Genesis 19:1.
7. "Jerusalem" is always seen as a type of the Church, and if the glory can come into the Church, then God can come into the nations as well.
8. See 1 Chronicles 15:24.
9. See 1 Chronicles 15:18.
10. See Acts 5:28.
11. Acts 19:10 NKJV.
12. Psalm 24:7 NKJV.
13. Psalm 134:1-2 NKJV.
14. Luke 11:52 NKJV.

Other *exciting titles* by Tommy Tenney

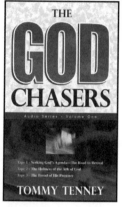

AUDIOTAPE ALBUMS BY TOMMY TENNEY

Order this

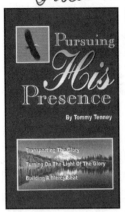

PURSUING HIS PRESENCE

(audiotape album) $20 plus $4.50 S&H

20.00
4.50
$24.50

Tape 1 - Transporting the Glory: The only thing that can carry "the ark" (the glory of God) is sanctification, the developing of godly character. Also learn about "divine radiation zones."

Tape 2 - Turning On the Light of the Glory: Tommy deals with turning on the light of the glory and presence of God, and he walks us through the necessary process and ingredients to potentially unleash what His Body has always dreamed of.

Tape 3 - Building a Mercy Seat: If we build the mercy seat—in the spiritual sense—according to the pattern that God gave to Moses, the same thing will happen as occurred when the original was built. The presence of God came and dwelt between the outstretched wings of the worshiping cherubim.

FANNING THE FLAMES

(audiotape album) $20 plus $4.50 S&H

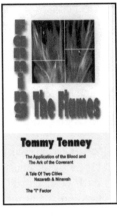

Tape 1 - The Application of the Blood and the Ark of the Covenant: Most of the churches in America today dwell in an outer-court experience. Jesus made atonement with His own blood, once for all, and the veil in the temple was rent from top to bottom.

Tape 2 - A Tale of Two Cities—Nazareth & Ninevah: Jesus spent more time in Nazareth than any other city, yet there was great resistance to the works of God there. In contrast, consider the characteristics of the people of Ninevah.

Tape 3 - The "I" Factor: Examine the difference between *ikabod* and *kabod* ("glory"). The arm of flesh cannot achieve what needs to be done. God doesn't need us; we need Him.

KEYS TO LIVING THE REVIVED LIFE

(audiotape album) $20 plus $4.50 S&H

Tape 1 - Fear Not: The principles that Tommy reveals teach us that to have no fear is to have faith, and that perfect love casts out fear, so we establish the trust of a child in our loving Father.

Tape 2 - Hanging In There: Have you ever been tempted to give up, quit, and throw in the towel? This message is a word of encouragement for you. Everybody has a place and a position in the Kingdom of God. Jeannie Tenney joins her husband and sings an inspiring chorus, "I'm going through."

Tape 3 - Fire of God: Fire purges the sewer of our souls and destroys the hidden things that would cause disease. Learn the way out of a repetitive cycle of seasonal times of failure.

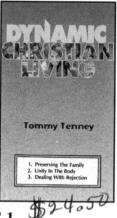

Destiny Image
New Releases

Other

Destiny Image **titles**
you will enjoy reading

FATHER, FORGIVE US!
by Jim W. Goll.
What is holding back a worldwide "great awakening"? What hinders the Church all over the world from rising up and bringing in the greatest harvest ever known? The answer is simple: sin! God is calling Christians today to take up the mantle of identificational intercession and repent for the sins of the present and past; for the sins of our fathers; for the sins of the nations. Will you heed the call? This book shows you how!
ISBN 0-7684-2025-3

AN INVITATION TO FRIENDSHIP: From the Father's Heart, Volume 2
by Charles Slagle.
Our God is a Father whose heart longs for His children to sit and talk with Him in fellowship and oneness. This second volume of intimate letters from the Father to you, His child, reveals His passion, dreams, and love for you. As you read them, you will find yourself drawn ever closer within the circle of His embrace. The touch of His presence will change your life forever!
ISBN 0-7684-2013-X

THE THRESHOLD OF GLORY
Compiled by Dotty Schmitt.
What does it mean to experience the "glory of God"? How does it come? These women of God have crossed that threshold, and it changed not only their ministries but also their very lives! Here Dotty Schmitt and Sue Ahn, Bonnie Chavda, Pat Chen, Dr. Flo Ellers, Brenda Kilpatrick, and Varle Rollins teach about God's glorious presence and share how it transformed their lives.
ISBN 0-7684-2044-X

THE HIDDEN POWER OF PRAYER AND FASTING
by Mahesh Chavda.
The praying believer is the confident believer. But the fasting believer is the overcoming believer. This is the believer who changes the circumstances and the world around him. He is the one who experiences the supernatural power of the risen Lord in his everyday life. An international evangelist and the senior pastor of All Nations Church in Charlotte, North Carolina, Mahesh Chavda has seen firsthand the power of God released through a lifestyle of prayer and fasting. Here he shares from decades of personal experience and scriptural study principles and practical tips about fasting and praying. This book will inspire you to tap into God's power and change your life, your city, and your nation!
ISBN 0-7684-2017-2

Available at your local Christian bookstore.

Internet: http://www.reapernet.com

Other
*Destiny Image **titles***
you will enjoy reading

A HEART FOR GOD
by Charles P. Schmitt.
This powerful book will send you on a 31-day journey with David from brokenness to wholeness. Few men come to God with as many millstones around their necks as David did. Nevertheless, David pressed beyond adversity, sin, and failure into the very forgiveness and deliverance of God. The life of David will bring hope to those bound by generational curses, those born in sin, and those raised in shame. David's life will inspire faith in the hearts of the dysfunctional, the failure-ridden, and the fallen!
ISBN 1-56043-157-1

SECRETS OF THE MOST HOLY PLACE
by Don Nori.
Here is a prophetic parable you will read again and again. The winds of God are blowing, drawing you to His Life within the Veil of the Most Holy Place. There you begin to see as you experience a depth of relationship your heart has yearned for. This book is a living, dynamic experience with God!
ISBN 1-56043-076-1

ENCOUNTERING THE PRESENCE
by Colin Urquhart.
What is it about Jesus that, when we encounter Him, we are changed? When we encounter the Presence, we encounter the Truth, because Jesus is the Truth. Here Colin Urquhart, best-selling author and pastor in Sussex, England, explains how the Truth changes facts. Do you desire to become more like Jesus? The Truth will set you free!
ISBN 0-7684-2018-0

Available at your local Christian bookstore.
Internet: http://www.reapernet.com